P9-BYX-384

CALVIN D. SUN, MD

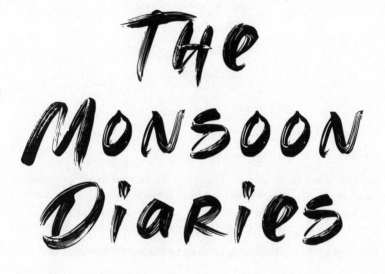

The MONSOON Diaries

A Doctor's Journey of Hope and
Healing from the ER Frontlines
to the Far Reaches of the World

HARPER HORIZON

*Dedicated to those no longer with us on this plane of physical
existence but who will always remain with us,
especially as long as you're remembered. We remember.*

Dad, Alexander S. Sun

Grandpa, Sheng-De Xu

Grandma, Lusa Sun

Everett Jiang

Sonia Sethi

The Monsoon Diaries

Copyright © 2022 Calvin D. Sun, MD

All rights reserved. No portion of this book may be reproduced, stored in a re-trieval system, or transmitted in any form or by any means—electronic, mechan-ical, photocopy, recording, scanning, or other—except for brief quotations in critical reviews or articles, without the prior written permission of the publisher.

Published by Harper Horizon, an imprint of HarperCollins Focus LLC.

Any internet addresses, phone numbers, or company or product information printed in this book are offered as a resource and are not intended in any way to be or to imply an endorsement by Harper Horizon, nor does Harper Horizon vouch for the existence, content, or services of these sites, phone numbers, com-panies, or products beyond the life of this book.

The information in this book has been carefully researched by the authors, and is intended to be a source of information only. Readers are urged to consult with their physicians or other professional advisors to address specific medical or other issues. The author and the publisher assume no responsibility for any in-juries suffered or damages incurred during or as a result of the use or applica-tion of the information contained herein.

ISBN 978-0-7852-9176-3 (Ebook)
ISBN 978-0-7852-9175-6 (HC)

Library of Congress Control Number: 2021953429

Printed in the United States of America
22 23 24 25 26 LSC 10 9 8 7 6 5 4 3 2 1

CONTENTS

FOREWORD

~~~~~~~

By Lisa Ling

This is a memoir unlike any I have read before. It reads as if Jack Kerouac were a roving ER doctor on the frontlines of a global pandemic for which healthcare systems the world over were totally unprepared. One minute I am venturing alongside a young man who loses himself in the far corners of the earth as he tries to discover himself and his purpose. The next, I am in the proverbial belly of the beast with him as he dives headfirst into an outbreak of apocalyptic proportions. This book is about how the intersection of these divergent worlds leads that man, Dr. Calvin Sun, to find his place and, ultimately, his voice.

Like most everyone in the beginning of the COVID-19 pandemic, when I was stuck at home with my device attached to me like an appendage, I spent endless hours scrolling for new information about the mysterious virus that had become rooted in our country. Refreshing my news feed to learn more about how the virus was ravaging New York City became an almost rote action. I watched every press conference; I read and reread everything posted online about the rapid spread of the new coronavirus. I followed anyone on social media who might have insights into that upon which our country was embarking.

One day as I was scouring my feed, I came across a cable news report that featured a very young-looking Asian American doctor. Dr. Calvin Sun looked like a kid in his twenties with what appeared to be a bruise on the top of his nose. I would later learn that it was, in fact, a bruise from wearing suction goggles for multiple consecutive twelve-hour shifts. It turned out Dr. Sun, a per diem New York City emergency room doctor, was thirty-three, but he spoke with a composure and urgency befitting of those I saw on daily network press conferences. But more than the others, I found myself glued to the way in which Dr. Sun described in explicit detail the scenes playing out in emergency rooms across the city. He talked about how as a per diem doctor, he can choose when and where he wants to work, but in a wartime scenario such as this, "it's a calling—I have to go in."

Amid the TV tickers bearing the numbers of the dead and infected, Dr. Sun spoke so commandingly, I could not help but take notice. I found him on Instagram (@monsoondiaries) and followed him immediately.

What are "monsoon diaries"? As I looked through Dr. Sun's feed, I got a glimpse of his prepandemic life. Baghdad. Islamabad. Chernobyl. Madagascar. Nauru. How was this young doctor able to travel to so many distant lands? How did he possibly have the time? I didn't have the energy to dig into the hows and whys; at the time, all I wanted to do was find out more about COVID-19. And frankly, colorful and adventurous travel seemed like something from a bygone era.

Nevertheless, Dr. Sun's feed became one of my go-to sources for information about what was happening inside hospitals and among healthcare workers. It was a portal and an aggregator for those inside to decry the horrors of what they were experiencing. And it became a battle cry and a declaration of how America's highly trained medical regiment was getting sent into an ambush mission without the armor or arms to engage perhaps the deadliest, most unpredictable aggressor the world has known. But through it all, Dr. Sun remained steadfast, undeterred, and utterly battle ready.

I never could have known in those early months of the pandemic, as I hung on to every word and every one of his posts, how travel to far-flung locations—or "monsooning," as he likes to call it—shaped and helped prepare him for what was to come. Dr. Sun spent the first half of his life trying to live up to impossible expectations and was gripped by impostor syndrome that forced him to question himself and what he was supposed to do with his life. But his incredible journey of taking a leap into the unknown and finding himself with no one else to rely on allowed him to reframe his fear into a resolve that led him to suit up and face down whatever lay before him.

There are heroes among us, and Dr. Calvin Sun is one of them. Read this book.

Lisa Ling
May 2022

PROLOGUE

~~~~~~~~~

March 26, 2020

"We have a code!"

"Make sure everyone's got all their PPE on!" I yell, running.

Habits take over. Hurry in. Handrails down. Begin CPR. Confirm roles. Wheel in crash cart. Push meds.

The resuscitation symphony begins. Ventilators chime. Monitors ring. Ribs crack. "Check pulse. Resume compressions." Otherwise, silence.

The other patients watch in horror. There's no space here to close privacy curtains, with stretchers and patients jammed into every spare inch of the emergency department, but out of instinct we try anyway. Our curtains then deliberately fight us by tangling themselves under the wheels of two separate gurneys.

Ah fuck the curtains, we'll work with an audience.

The whole world has been our audience.

Hospital administrators informed us earlier this week that in order to do the greatest good for the greatest number of people, we won't be able to do everything for everyone. But habits are hard to break. Some of us will try to do it all any-way. It's all we know how to do.

The habit of adrenaline kicks in and emotions betray logic. *Maybe I do like this. Maybe I still have a purpose.*

No. How could you like this? You're living a never-ending disaster.

OK. I hate this more than I like it.

I continue to give orders to my team, running the code even as I take stock of my own PPE too late to do anything about it; out of a delayed reflex I then reach for my fore-head . . .

Oh whoops.

No. Not "Oh whoops": It's a bona fide "Oh fuck." Not again: I don't have any eye coverings on. *Goner.* Like Brendan Glee-son's character Frank in *28 Days Later* when a drop of zombie blood falls in his eye, that moment when you realize a new inevitable can feel so unfair . . . *Whatever, too late now, can't turn back time, got to do your best for him.* Looking at this patient, I feel as if I'm now looking at my own future twenty-eight days later. *You're still standing and he's not, don't worry about what hasn't happened yet, do what you can until it's your turn on the stretcher.* I almost throw my hands up in the air, but the best I can muster is a sigh and a frown.

Get yourself back in there. Your code is to run this code.

I continue: Keep pushing on his chest. Keep giving him those breaths.

Pulse check: *pulse, pulse, pulse.* We got him back; I stop the code. He's alive for now. Are we alive? I check my own: *pulse pulse pulse pulse pulse pulse.* It's faster than the patient's. I need to breathe, too, so I consciously slow mine down: *in . . . out . . . in . . . out . . .* Pulses and breaths have become valuable com-modities these days.

I call out and remind everyone: Wash your hands, spray yourselves down, and change your PPE . . . if there's any left to change into. Everybody returns to what they were doing before, taking no notice of the panicky whites of my uncovered eyes. I don't blame them. They have their own worries.

Who cares for the carer?

The patient's nurse informs me that he was actually admitted yesterday but has waited down here in the ER for more than twenty-five hours for a bed that doesn't exist. His doctor, the hospitalist upstairs, needs to be informed. I call and update him about the code, then call the patient's family. His prognosis is grim. They understand.

My prognosis is grim. *No eye coverings, fuck.*

You will never be able to stop this.

Maybe I should just quit.

Get back in there.

Get me out of here.

I shake off the dueling voices of my subconscious as the respiratory therapist arrives with the hospital's last ventilator.

"Any new vents like they promised?" I ask, referring to Governor Cuomo's assurances that more mechanical ventilators to help patients breathe are coming from a national stockpile, and trying to distract myself from my potential exposure to the virus that is killing people before my very uncovered eyes.

"No, we're the leftovers," he says with a dark grin. I know what he means: Not all hospitals are created equal, and this one is less equal than most.

The hospitalist from upstairs comes down to see the patient for himself. Within minutes, the man goes into cardiac arrest again. It's now the hospitalist's turn to run the code. He, at least, remembers to have his eye coverings on.

"Start chest compressions! Get me an epi!"

I try to be helpful in the role reversal and dial the patient's family again. They pick up immediately, knowing another call this soon can mean only one thing. They don't want to replay this horror scene again and again, so they tell me it's time to let him go naturally. In peace. Away from us.

I walk over to inform the hospitalist, who's continuing compressions, and he gets on the phone for a double confirmation. A few seconds later he calls off the code. "Family confirmed the DNR. I'm calling it."

He pronounces time of death, 9:03 p.m., nods at me, and starts his run back upstairs . . . where another code is being called. "We might have an open bed soon," he says darkly. His run is a zombie shamble. I notice his exhaustion, then he's gone.

The patient will stay downstairs with us, alone, until he can be moved to the morgue. *I've spent more time among the dead and dying lately than with my own friends. The dead are my new friends. Will I miss them when they're gone?* What kind of nightmares would I have if I weren't already living in one?

I give his family on the phone a number for the hospital's social workers as I scan the room. They couldn't physically squeeze in here even if pandemic protocols allowed for it. Before I can hang up, the next call comes:

"We've have a code!"

Habits take over. The resuscitation symphony plays again.

• • •

During many a late night after a shift, I sat shell-shocked in front of a screen—whether of a phone or a monitor—

mindlessly scrolling for information that did not yet exist. Spending months on the uncharted waters of the first pandemic of our generation, we struggled with how this was not something anyone could easily Google or Wikipedia their way out of. Whatever little we knew about this virus on the frontline was already more than anything you could find online.

If they're not of the pandemic, recurring nightmares still fool me into believing I'm back in college or medical school, and I had totally forgotten about a course or exam I needed to study for all year. Even after startling myself awake to reassure myself that the syndrome of feeling like an imposter back in school should long be over, an insecurity remains over whether I may have missed something that could have altered an outcome for the better. Another life that could have been saved.

If we could not be as confident of the outcome for any of our patients during this pandemic, how could we fully ascertain the risk of whether *we* would come out of this unscathed? And once it struck me there was no guarantee we would make it out of the pandemic alive either, I began to write.

I wrote not for you, but for me. I wrote by habit.

Or, if the worst were to happen, I wrote for whomever would be left to pick up the pieces and try to make sense of it all. Every moment put to virtual paper was confirmation, an affirmation to myself, that I was still alive.

This happened. These moments, captured on a break by hasty thumbs or recalled in my apartment after a death-washed double shift, happened. I lived them. I lived through them. I live to write this.

I write to live this.

I have a right to live.

Now that these moments are memory, and we look to-gether on what we survived and toward whatever comes next, I think I was writing for *us* all along.

For now, we've made it.

The first wave of our pandemic is no longer pointing a gun at our heads. Let's go forth and live.

PRODROME

~~~~~~~

February 24–March 7, 2020

n. (prō·drŏm) an early sign or symptom

that indicates the onset of disease.

The gun is pointed at my head.

Staring through a face shield into his goggles, my eyes lock with his.

Beep.

I survive the invisible bullet, my body temperature normal, and proceed to passport control, past a conspicuous sign (see next page) I can't read but have little trouble puzzling out.

Posted prominently (but only in Portuguese) for the handful of tourists arriving in Angola's only major international airport, that sign is already more than anything I'd seen the night before when leaving the United States. Public health authorities in a developing southwestern African nation are apparently more concerned than those in Washington, DC, about the spread of "coronavirus influenza," which I had overheard being uttered back home just before departing. (That is a combination of two different viruses, by the way, so make up your mind: which one is it?) The folks in Angola, at least, appear to believe it poses a valid threat. There are

ubiquitous temperature checks, hand sanitizers, and medical screeners armored in head-to-toe personal protective equipment (PPE). The best our own officials back home can muster are a couple of press releases on "monitoring the situation."

Following through on an invitation made months ago by a friend from the Netherlands named Rik, with whom I have occasionally co-led trips ever since we visited Venezuela together in 2015, I spend the next two weeks with his group of travelers in Angola. I learn more during that time about the spread of SARS-CoV-2 from their state-owned TV news than I had from all the independent media in my own country. There are updates each day on new places in the world where the virus has been identified; with each new report, my gut burns hotter for an early return home. But that's easier wished for than done in a young nation less than two decades out from a three-decade civil war.

One evening at dinner by Kalandula Falls in the lush Malanje Province, one of the Dutch travelers in our group asks me to examine him because of a toothache. I take a look and, sure enough, there is significant swelling that suggests infection. I advise him on antibiotics and to see an oral surgeon as soon as possible to drain the collection underneath, but after inquiring about alternate travel possibilities or even medical evacuation, we are told the earliest he could leave is on our already-scheduled flight out.

One of us in the group—we call ourselves "monsooners"—reassures him by reframing the situation, determined to enjoy what's left of the trip. "We're probably safer here anyway with that new virus out there."

I am left to ponder the irony.

• • •

As the day of our departure from Angola approaches, I do my usual before a long-haul flight: load up on music. But this time I also download recent medical podcasts on the illness now dubbed COVID-19, to hear how some of my colleagues are thinking about treating the virus and our potential exposure as healthcare providers.

One expresses a sentiment that turns me cold inside: "We're about to enter a lottery none of us wants to play."

I also download New York State's ventilator allocation guidelines, which has been a public document available online since 2015. Reading its 272 pages is not for the faint of heart, discussing as it does in minute detail what protocols to follow in the "extremely unlikely" event that patients ever overwhelm hospitals to the degree that ventilators must be rationed. The pandemic has barely gotten rolling, not really at least, and I'm already preparing for the worst—never imagining that the worst is exactly what's to come.

We arrive in Frankfurt where I part ways with Michael, whom I befriended on the trip. We give each other a final hug goodbye, knowing it would be one of our very last as such an act between fellow travelers would soon become a casualty of the virus.

Passing time on my layover, I then commit an infographic to memory:

Recommendations for COVID-19 Intubation

DO

- Wear an N95 mask

- Don fluid-resistant gowns, gloves, and face shields

- Use isolation rooms with negative-pressure

- Rapid Sequence Intubation

DON'T

- Don't initiate high-flow oxygen (including BIPAP, nebulizers, high flow nasal cannula, etc.)

- Don't permit any non-critical staff inside the room

- If possible, refrain from bagging the patient

- Don't allow any reason to prolong intubation attempt (DO use the most qualified provider with the quickest technique)

- Don't allow used PPE to leave the room (unless appropriately discarded)

I've spent the past two weeks traveling through a region still recovering from a civil war, and yet at least some part of me feels that returning home may be the greater danger.

I land at Newark Liberty International Airport at 5:00 p.m. on March 7, 2020. "Welcome Home!" is the only sign I see.

14 YEARS AGO

Summer 2006: Taking the Reins

A teenager's mind is a dangerous place to call home. It straddles the jagged line between childhood and the adult world, at once cocky and vulnerable, determined to "fake it till you make it" even as a lifetime of imposter syndrome sets in, sometimes so overwhelmed by its discovery of cognitive dissonance and the color of brumous gray that it freezes up and inclines itself toward self-destruction.

I can't help but feel I'm mishandling this grief over my father's death. One minute I'm still grateful to be alive at the age of nineteen, the next I feel radioactive, a danger to everyone around me, as though puberty is happening all over again. My frontal lobe, responsible for rational thinking and critical judgment, has been taken offline for unscheduled maintenance.

Three weeks ago, my father and I got into another shouting match. I then stormed off to my work in Washington Heights while he headed for stress relief at a New York Sports Club. A few hours later I would receive a phone call from a paramedic who tried to deliver the news that my father may have suddenly collapsed while on a treadmill and was found on the floor in cardiac arrest. But all I could hear was my mother's screams in the background.

After returning from the Emergency Room at Saint Vincent's Hospital later that night, my mother—who also had recently been formally diagnosed with Parkinson's disease—left to stay with her parents. I would return home alone.

I still wonder how I slept and what I could have dreamed of that night.

My father died three weeks ago.

He is gone.

I recall still returning to work in a numb daze the next morning. But later that afternoon my brother arrived to keep me company. Then my uncle and cousin. Then my aunt and uncle-in-law. Then two more of my cousins. Then my girlfriend at the time. In one week, the apartment was a hive; at least a dozen individuals were eating and sleeping and living together. I no longer felt as alone.

The last time all of us had come together was when we held a funeral for my paternal grandmother only three years prior, as if mourning rather than celebration had become a family tradition. And already having had two funerals so close together, I'm compelled to accept that on a long enough timeline we are only memories, feeling as real as imaginations of a little sister I would never get to grow up with.

At the funeral, when my brother assured me in front of everyone that our father truly was proud of me, I cried harder than I've ever done in my life. A few days later at a memorial service in New Haven where he had worked, his secretary pinned me to the wall with her eyes and said, "You're *that* son, right? The one who never stops arguing with him?"

"I guess that's me," I confirmed with an awkward shrug. Half-distracting myself with the soggy plate of food in my hand, I prepared myself for the worst but also did my best to hide that I was desperate to hear what she would say.

"After your arguments, where we could hear your screaming phone calls through the walls, he would slam down the phone and come out pacing and upset. But after a few minutes, he'd crack a smile and admit he admired you for standing up to him and never backing down . . . even though he felt that you were always wrong. He told me never to tell you, but I think you should know. He was . . . he still *is* proud of you."

If I am Sisyphus, my father was the boulder. My entire life I pushed against the weight of him, his expectations, his plans for me. He would be terrifying in trying to control my future, and I will never forget his volcanic eruptions of disappointment whenever I would express an alternative opinion.

In the rare times when he did soften, he would take me to the movies. I determined that in his struggle to communicate with me, and in lieu of the emotional support I would have needed from a father, he instead relied on the convenience of silently watching a movie together. So on the weekends when he returned home from his work in Connecticut, and whether we went to the theater on East 86th or East 64th Street, the movie would be followed by a ritual half-mile stroll back to our apartment with his hand on my right shoulder. Sometimes during these walks he stopped at the Papaya King for a quart of mango-papaya juice to take home, showed off his skills at fruit shopping by tapping on the best sounding melon, or tried to muster up a conversation in an attempt to tell me something, but most of the time he stayed silent. I don't ask for much . . . but I may have needed more from our relationship than

Sisyphus and his silent boulder trying to communicate a love language that became lost in translation.

Now the boulder has vanished and I'm stumbling over myself, nothing but the empty air of inadequacy, insecurity, and a lifetime desire for validation to hold my weight. We argued, I left, he got on a treadmill to blow off some steam and died. What do I do now, without his hand on my shoulder, the gravity of his immensity? How will I know what *not* to do, if I can't mutiny out of habit against his militant insistence that I must be a doctor? While I still tap on certain fruit and listen before I buy, I no longer enjoy the taste of mango-papaya juice.

Exactly two weeks after his death, everyone had to return to their own lives. And in what felt like a sudden turnaround, I was back to where I started the day he died. Alone for the first time in the apartment after two weeks of social overload, I waded in the irony of homesickness, a Welsh *hiraeth*, realizing how once again I had taken the brief company I enjoyed on this plane of existence for granted. I took my dad for granted. I took for granted all the support I'd had in the past two weeks. I felt like a deserted island: All I had was myself. I was on my own again. While it appeared as if ultimately nothing had changed before and after those two weeks, I knew that everything had. And nobody was going to answer those questions for me other than myself.

. . .

Tomorrow my fateful summer ends and my junior year back at Columbia begins, as I leave behind a home haunted by the memory of a family. I know life moves in only one direction, but the longing to go back in time is strong. I yearn for the days when school bus rides were a chance to crank up the latest Jimmy Eat World CD on my Discman and thus to deal with my massive-feeling problems. The days when family was a given, love was merely infatuation, and friendship was convenient for the most of us. I want that easy innocence again. Instead I'll take away the nostalgia of simple phone calls to check how I am doing, just like I used to get back in high school. And just as it had been then, I shall remain fiercely loyal to you.

I think it's time for a stroll.

You can walk 1.7 miles straight down Broadway from Columbia, past my high school, and end up at the 79th Street crosstown bus for the ride back to my childhood home. If you synchronize your pace with the traffic lights, you can do it without stopping. If you're lucky, a tailwind off the Hudson River will keep you company as you stride through my life in reverse.

They say you can find solace after a loss simply by ambling the streets of New York. Solve by walking. Today I wish I could do the same. I want the comfort of the known, even knowing how I have struggled against it. Against him. I wanted independence so fiercely, wanted him to finally hand over the reins of my life. Now that they're in my hands, how will I know what to do with them?

My heart heavy and weighed down doubly by the taste of summer humidity, I struggle to catch my breath. I walk down these familiar streets feeling more alone, choking on uncertainty.

PYREXIA

~~~~~~~~

March 8–18, 2020

n. (pī·rek·sē·uh) abnormal elevation

of body temperature; fever.

MARCH 8, 2020

My lungs taste the brisk winter air as I wave down a cab at 6:15 a.m. For some reason Trent Reznor and Atticus Ross's track "Hand Covers Bruise" is buzzing in my head as we pass the dim lights of a still-slumbering New York City. My hometown lies asleep under the tender maw of an Henri Rousseau lion.

Forty minutes later I arrive for my 7:00 a.m. shift at an ER in Brooklyn.

• • •

I don't work for just one hospital. I'm a per diem doctor by choice. Once I discovered monsooning (or did it discover me?)—whether it was by luck or kismet just before medical school—I had to find a way to be both a doctor and a frequent traveler. Per diem shifts enable me to keep up a rigorous (some, wrongly, would snide as "ridiculous") pace of international travel while also practicing emergency medicine: the rapid diagnosis, treatment, and disposition of people likely having one of, if not the worst day of their lives.

The calling of an ER doctor is to see all patients regardless of gender, race, creed, culture, religion, language, social status, or ability to pay—usually with only a minimum of background information—in the limited time at our disposal. We see all kinds of medical requests from patients such as those who simply need a note for work without wanting a medical exam, to mass casualty incidents. At our best we diagnose, stabilize, and begin treatment for potentially life- or limb-threatening conditions. In those particular cases, our job is akin to time distortion: We do all we can to expand the seconds or minutes before death or a permanently debilitating condition, stretching those moments with our timely interventions into hours, days, even weeks. With newly leased time, we can transfer the patient to more specialized care, or work out a safe plan to send them home to follow up with another specialist or their primary care physician—hopefully forestalling the worst altogether.

The science of medicine isn't perfect, and neither are our expectations. We go into each day knowing that, despite our training, we're never 100 percent prepared for any shift we sign up for. Half the battle is showing up.

• • •

So here I show up in Brooklyn, at one of New York City's dozens of hospitals that need per diem emergency physicians for sufficient coverage. I "take sign-out" from the doctor who worked the night shift, which means I will receive follow-up instructions for his patients still in the emergency room and who are waiting for the results of their tests, before we decide to either recommend them admission to the hospital or a discharge back home. I scan the board that lists the symptoms of those waiting to be seen. It's mostly the usual assortment of aches, pains, and injuries, but one less familiar word floats next to three different names: *exposure.*

They are people with no symptoms who want to be tested for coronavirus.

"Someone next to me on the subway was coughing."

"A neighbor down the hall is sick."

"I know someone who's sick and I feel tired."

But we have no tests, no way to confirm or rule out the presence of the virus. All we have in this emergency room are flu and strep throat tests. Not even a day into a burgeoning pandemic, and I already wanted to get on top of a podium and announce: *These are not the tests you're looking for.* This is a day when, despite our training, we are 100 percent not 100 percent prepared.

What is the next month going to be like?

My team puts our heads together to jury-rig this conundrum and someone suggests we swab all three patients for influenza A and B. If they come up positive, we can assume it's not COVID and provide them recommendations for flu care. And yet something in the back of my mind wants to raise its hand: *What if they can have both influenza and the coronavirus? And what if the flu tests come back negative?* They look at me and I shrug as if this was already looking more like a jerry-rig than a jury-rig.

So let's take an extra swab from each patient and send it over to the NYC Department of Health with a request for sequencing on an available polymerase chain reaction (PCR) machine: the best way to confirm infection of SARS-CoV-2. And yet deep down I fear our Department of Health is as much in the dark as we are. In a few hours, they'll probably be inundated by random samples from all over the city from clueless healthcare workers like us who don't know what else to do besides kick it up the ladder.

I also tell the staff to make sure patients without symptoms leave as soon as possible after their swabs. If they do have coronavirus, we don't want them loitering in a cramped ER breathing all over everyone else, including us. And if they don't have it, we don't want them lingering around to breathe *in* the coronavirus or any other pathogen common to big-city ERs in wintertime. God forbid they get sick because they came here hoping *not* to be sick. In my mind's eye, I already foresee patients lying stretcher to stretcher like *Tetris* gone horribly wrong, sharing thick air saturated with multiple viruses jockeying for their next victim, as more and sicker people line up in the waiting room jockeying for a chance to be one of them. My inner doomsayer zooms out to take in all the people those sick people will infect getting to and from the ER: neighbors, bus drivers, train conductors, fellow passengers, taxi drivers, people on the street . . .

We've got to get these people home.
We've got to get everyone else to stay home.

Right about then I begin to consider my staff's need for better respiratory protection. I recall the main titles scene to *Outbreak* and ask a hospital administrator about a powered-air purifying respirator, a PAPR, which makes the wearer look like an astronaut.

"That . . . mechanical helmet thing? We might have one, but it's probably locked in a storage room somewhere." *So a Hollywood movie from 1995 is already way more accurate and ahead of us on this pandemic.*

I don't have time to hunt down something that may or may not exist except in the childhood memory of a movie nearly a quarter-century old. "Okay, where are the N95s then?"

"If they're not already in the ER, check central supply."

Twenty minutes are gone before I'm able to track down a dusty, half-empty box of old N95 filtered masks. *Twenty minutes when I could have discharged patients before they catch something.*

"Are these all the N95s we have?"

Eventually I get an answer from central supply: "That's what we have for the rest of the week."

I'm incredulous. "For the whole week? For all of us? Are you kidding?"

I receive the generic backup response: "Supply chain issues."

Every year they test us on properly fitting these things. Isn't the whole point that one day our lives will depend on checking that compliance box?

I put one on and then take it off, as if I were relearning how to ride a bike—our new habit for at least the next few months. Then, clutching my already wilted, coffee-stained N95, I can't help but now remember the Klendathu invasion scene in *Starship Troopers*, where soldiers of a newly minted mobile infantry battalion expend massive time and effort to neutralize a single enemy combatant only to look up and see hundreds of thousands more swarming the horizon. This mask was designed to be worn for a single patient encounter. What about the swarm of patients just off camera?

"Your mask looks special," says my first potential coronavirus patient.

"This? Yeah, it's called an N95 mask."

"N95?"

"Yeah, it filters the air I breathe better than a regular mask. And because it's possible anyone can be carrying an easily transmissible virus right now, I want to avoid being exposed, both for my own health and for the sake of the people I'll see after you."

"Do you have any extras?" he asks. I did not expect this. "I'll just take some with me, if that's okay."

"I'm afraid we don't. I just spent twenty minutes looking for this and found one half-empty box. That may be all we have for the rest of the week."

His eyes narrow. "That doesn't sound right; this is a hospital. You just don't want to give them to me."

I narrow my eyes to match. "I would be happy to give you some masks if we had a surplus, but we don't. That's the truth."

"Give me a box right now," he demands.

Patient's testing my patience.

"Sir, the longer you stay here and get into this with me, the longer you're going to expose yourself—and others—to all the pathogens each person has brought in with them. You don't need an N95 right now at this moment because one, we even as healthcare workers don't have enough, and two, I'm going to advise you to quarantine at home. If *we* get sick, there will be no one to take care of you and your loved ones when *you* get sick."

I offer him a regular surgical mask and step outside, only to see him slip down the hall with two pilfered boxes of surgical masks, plus a bonus box of latex gloves, tucked under his arm. *If an acute wave of coronavirus infections won't kill us, an acute wave of entitlement will.* Whether out of habit or frustration, I've just ripped off my single-use N95 to toss it, but then realized if we change between each patient our pitiful supply won't even last the shift—let alone the rest of the week. I guess I'll hold on to this one until I know I can get my hands on another. *I'm not going to let that patient have the satisfaction of killing me.*

So I take my soiled N95 mask home, just in case.

One minute's trash is another minute's treasure.

MARCH 9, 2020

My second day back from Angola, I arrive for a 4:00 p.m. shift with my now one-day-old N95 in hand. Parked outside the ER is a Medical Evacuation Transportation Unit fire truck. I've never seen one and half hope, even while knowing better, that it's for something other than the coronavirus.

Inside I glance at the electronic board and see:

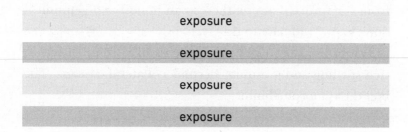

exposure

exposure

exposure

exposure

exposure
exposure
exposure

Seven patients, all asymptomatic, had come in at once, all here to be tested for the virus. But nothing has changed in twenty-four hours: We still have no tests. We swab them for existing viral panels as quickly as possible and take an extra sample each to send over to the Department of Health, still hoping someone there will have more answers.

I've always thought that one of our main jobs as healthcare workers is to guide our patients through the dense nebula of sickness and health, helping them better understand what they're experiencing when no one else can. We never have *all* the answers, but we usually have enough.

Not today.

Even though we swore to the fifth verse of the modern version of the Hippocratic Oath to feel no shame over saying "I know not," today uttering the words "I don't know" to a patient has never felt so unforgivable.

I remind myself that anyone out there right now who claims to truly know what's going on with a virus only a few months old is either lying to themselves or a time traveler from the future. I am neither, so an honest and genuine "I don't know" will have to do.

Two hours later, eight new patients have come in so fast that spelling and grammar become collateral damage. The board has morphed into:

diagnosed with **coronavirus**
tested positive for coronavirus, denies symptoms
tested positive for coronavirus, denies symptoms
tested positive for coronavirus, denies symptoms
diagnosed with coronavirus
tested positive for coronavirus, denies symptoms
tested positive for coronavirus, Pt have fever & chill
coronavirus dx

My mind is whirling with more questions than ever. *There are tests available now? Where? And if these patients are actually positive, why are they here when they have no symptoms? What are we supposed to do with them?*

I know there's more fear than malice behind people's decisions to come here unnecessarily, but I still want to shake them from this nightmare, wake them up, and make them take a closer look at the older, more vulnerable patients in the chairs next to them. They sit in a waiting room with no windows to circulate fresh air, with each breath from each person sealing everyone else's fate. (I will find out late in the day that many of these people were exposed to the first cluster of patients in Westchester, and shudder when I imagine all the future patients they may have created by coming all the way to Brooklyn. *So this is how a zombie movie starts.*)

One patient has normal vital signs and an oxygen saturation rate of 100 percent. He says, "I got a call saying I tested positive, so I'm here for a second opinion. But I feel fine."

Having overheard this, there is muttering from other patients, "Jesus, why are you here? Are you kidding?"

I feel my patience already wearing thin. I motion to my staff to make sure everyone in the waiting room including security is wearing a mask, just in case things get dicey.

"Sir, if you tested positive for something so new there's no cure for it yet, if you say you feel fine and have no symptoms, if your vital signs are well within normal limits and you're supposed to be quarantined at home, then you're endangering every person here for a second opinion." That's when I notice he isn't even wearing a mask. The registrar had just come by to offer him one, but he waved her away. "Just because you don't have symptoms doesn't mean you're not spreading coronavirus to me, my staff, and all these other patients. You've already tested positive!"

"Why won't you test me again?" he asks, ignoring everything I've said. The first stage of grief is denial. But I'm stuck: At least in zombie movies the protagonists get a chance to cut and run first before getting cornered.

That's when some of the other waiting patients stand up. I don't know if they're ready to leave or to punch him in the face (after which he would have a legitimate reason to be here).

"We don't have tests, but even if we did, you can't test a virus away. How can you live with yourself, knowing you've tested positive and then coming here to spread it? Without even the barest courtesy of wearing a mask?"

He tries one last time. Bargaining. "I'm not leaving until you test me again."

"For the last time, *sir*, knowingly spreading a pathogen is, at the very least, manslaughter. *Someone in this room next to you will probably die* because you came here today. If you don't leave now, I will call security to escort you out and call the police to arrest you for trespassing and possibly assault since you're refusing to put on a mask. Go home!"

Anger. "Can I speak to your supervisor?"

"I *am* the supervisor. Leave now." *Acceptance.* Deal with it.

I call over security and stalk off to see my next patient, leaving the first to the fury of the waiting room.

MARCH 11, 2020

"Can you pick up a shift today, Calvin?" While walking with my friends around Nolita, I get a last-minute call from an ER in the area.

"Oh boy . . . you're lucky I'm actually nearby and happen to have my stethoscope on me, but only if it's okay for me to see patients in my jeans and wearing a jacket from another hospital?"

"Sure," he replied. Usually he tells me to turn the jacket inside-out, but today, he said, "We had a doctor just call out sick. Come as you are as soon as you can."

This ER is in a more affluent area than the one I've been in the past few days, so I'm able to hide my dressed-down appearance upon arrival with a proper surgical gown, a new N95, splash-guard eyewear, and even a face shield. *New PPE! Such a luxury.* I feel good, thrilled in fact, to reset my N95 stopwatch. *These disposable goggles are sweet! Gotta hold on to these.*

My first patient has flu-like symptoms. She looks feverish and dehydrated and says she's scared that it's "that virus I heard about on the news." I try to reassure her, but find as I coordinate with the team that, even here in Manhattan with its relatively greater resources, nobody definitively knows where her nasal swabs should go either. We therefore "do them all" and send one downstairs to the on-site lab, one to the Department of Health, and one to LabCorp, which we've heard has been contracted for its PCR machines. A few hours later, her in-house swab comes back positive for influenza A, and her oxygen saturation is holding at 99 percent, so I send her home with flu precautions. But God only knows if there's such thing as a co-infection with COVID-19, and I don't intend to keep her in an emergency room for the two days it would take to find out.

But there's nothing here like the crowding in Brooklyn. At least in Manhattan, patients are staying away, as the TV talking heads have instructed.

An administrator comes by around 8:00 p.m. and says, "If you haven't heard, the WHO just declared this a pandemic and released guidelines for COVID isolation. By their guidelines, we're downgrading our protocols from airborne to droplet precautions."

I protest, "But the virus could still spread in the air! Maybe we should err on the safe side and keep airborne precautions to contain the spread. We're talking actual life and death here."

"I know and I agree with you," he admits. "But we don't have enough negative pressure rooms to enforce airborne precautions for a pandemic-level virus."

"Droplet precautions." We might as well be working through a thick tropical fog.

. . .

At most of the hospitals I've worked in, there are, at most, one or two rooms with negative pressure capabilities, where special vents suck out and filter the air so that it's as clean as if the isolated patient were on a plane or in a subway by themselves. These one or two rooms could maybe handle a "surge" of one or two patients and their exposed families per day for an airborne virus such as measles or SARS. Since it's rare these days for a patient to waltz through the door with measles, one or two rooms has always been enough.

But if authorities officially designate this novel coronavirus as both pandemic-level *and* airborne—which would require airborne isolation precautions—hospital systems would likely go bankrupt on the spot, either shutting down for months or spending billions to retrofit all their facilities with enough negative pressure rooms to handle a surge that is already on its way.

I reckon that an arbitrary move of the goalposts without sufficient evidence at this point of the pandemic—downgrading the virus's behavior to droplet spread rather than airborne—will allow healthcare workers to stick multiple afflicted patients with masks on in one droplet isolation room, and *maybe* keep pace with a pandemic-level surge.

I hope we can live with the decisions we're making today.

MARCH 12, 2020

A different ER in uptown Manhattan today. "Can I get a coronavirus test?" the patient asks. He's an older man, maybe in his eighties. No symptoms.

"Were you exposed?" I ask.

"I think so. I saw a guy in my building an hour ago who was coughing across the lobby . . ." He tries to look me in the eye but can't quite get there. "He's Asian."

"Oh," I say. This is new. "Hmm. And were you . . . close to him?"

I let my words, eyes, and the following silence sink in. His wife then buries her face in her hands, obviously wanting to hide from her shock of his delivery and embarrassment. "Oh my God, I'm so sorry, Doctor," she says, muffled apologies slipping through her fingers.

In times of crisis, when fear of the unknown short-circuits the frontal lobe's receptors for empathy, a fragile ego's desire for self-preservation renders anything "different" or "foreign" to be the scapegoat: people of color, people of faith, sexual and ethnic minorities, scientists, those who discovered Earth actually revolves around the sun, or healthcare workers who discover new viruses, treatments, and preventions. Why, after so many posthumous acquittals, do we still fear the witches more than the mobs who burn them alive? Or worse, the crowds that stand there and do nothing?

This man is in my ER because he is afraid. I get that. He acts out and then responds as he does because he is afraid. But also, *wow*.

I hope this isn't a sign of things to come.

"Let's go, Walter," the wife says, standing and pulling at his arm. She can't meet my eyes as she drags him away, but at the door she turns and says, "Thank you for all you're doing and please stay safe, Doctor."

MARCH 13, 2020

In the Bronx today. Droves of patients looking for tests. They seem sicker here. What a difference a day and a borough can make, I guess. In-hospital SARS-CoV-2 tests have arrived, but they still take a few days to return results. Less than ideal, but better than nothing.

A forty-year-old woman presents with flu-like symptoms and a history of congestive heart failure, showing her oxygen saturation at a consistent 85 percent—dangerously low for someone of her age and history. She was exposed by one of the original Westchester patients, a confirmed case, but here today she looks . . . well, fine, actually, and her lung exam is clear with no wheezing or crackles. And she says she *feels* fine, no shortness of breath, just scared.

On a normal day we are not comfortable with oxygen levels below 90 to 92 percent, no matter how well the patient speaks in complete sentences. Thinking out loud, I suggest the need for preemptive intubation, which would mean having a breathing tube inserted in her throat so a machine can breathe for her and keep her oxygen levels up. To be intubated would mean being sedated and paralyzed into a medical coma. It's called "invasive ventilation" for good reason.

But she knows what intubation would mean and is soon sitting bolt upright, first texting and then talking frantically with her mother, crying. I start preparing myself and the team for my first intubation of a patient with presumed COVID-19. This ER, unlike the one in Manhattan yesterday, does not have proper face shields that rest over the forehead and fully cover the face from above. Instead there are flimsy plastic shields jutting up from paper surgical masks that leave the entire top of the head exposed. I'm regretting throwing out the single-use shield I got in Manhattan. *At least I kept the goggles.*

Time feels short. I don't want to risk her oxygen saturation dropping further, but when I look over she's still on the phone, clearly not short of breath. I also don't want to rush her potentially life-changing decision. So I scrabble around the ER, on the hunt for more PPE. In addition to the flimsy shield-plus-mask on the bottom half of my face, I tie another upside down above my forehead with the shield pointing down, essentially jury-rigging a full-face shield. It looks like a Venus flytrap has just clamped down on my face as if I were its prey. To the bottom mask around my neck, I tape a plastic garbage bag–like gown, and then add a hairnet for good measure. *This is getting ridiculous.*

She's still on the phone, talking in full and complete sentences and gesturing emphatically. *How can this be happening? How can someone with saturation levels that low talk more in fifteen minutes than I do on an average day?*

I realize that, in all my experience as an emergency physician, I have intubated patients only in "clinical extremis"— tripoding forward with their arms on their knees or the stretcher with air hunger, falling in and out of consciousness, struggling for coherent words as their brains are deprived of oxygen, exhausted from breathing too fast with too little result. In other words, I have never even considered intubating someone who looks and sounds like this patient. If not for the number on the oxygen monitor, nothing about her warrants the need for a breathing tube. *Is this the right move, clinically? Is intubation really what's best for her? Am I intubating a person or a number? Is there such thing as a right answer at this point of the pandemic?*

She ends the call with her mother and waves me over. "I want to sign out. I want to leave against medical advice." It feels as if she has said something like this before.

I walk her through some confirmatory questions. Does she understand that she could die, walking out with an 85 percent oxygen level and a history of heart failure? Yes, and with more lucidity than anyone with those levels should exhibit. When oxygen levels drop, we expect an altered mental state that would preclude these kinds of decisions. But right here in front of us is a patient who can demonstrate she knows the risks of both choices and is making a clear-eyed decision to walk out of here on her own. She even preemptively asks for the forms to sign and says she'll arrange for her primary doctor to send her some home oxygen. She is determined to leave. As she heads for the door, she calls her mom for a ride.

For her sake, I hope she never has to come back.

"Where's my fucking COVID test?" yells a patient in triage.

MARCH 14, 2020

Back in Brooklyn. A field tent is being set up just outside the front entrance. Ambulances roll up one after another, rarely a break between sirens, and the walk-in line only grows, even as we process patients as fast as humanly possible.

The war metaphors write themselves.

At 8:32 a.m., the board looks like this:

Cough

Cough, Sore Throat

Cough

Cough

Fever

Nasal Congestion; Fever

Cough

Cough; Nasal Congestion

Cough; Fever

Cough; Fever

Cough Sore Throat Headache

Cough; Fever

Cough/Cold/Fever

Cough; Fever

Fever, sore throat

Other

Shortness of Breath; Cough

Cough

Cough

Fever; Cough

Chest Pain; Cough

Cough; Nasal Congestion

Cough; Fever
Cough; Fever
Cough
Cough
Fever; Cough

Glancing at headlines and the waiting room TV on my way in, my mind wants to distract itself from real and present horror with more philosophical pursuits. What was it like the last time a world war started? *Well, the lead-up to World War II had a lot in common with this shit show: denial, fear, exploitation of fear, ambivalence, complacency, political machinations, propaganda, misinformation, uncertainty, entitlement. Can we avoid friendly fire, violence, and death?*

Wasn't the last most severe pandemic in recent history during the First World War?

I shake myself out of escapist gloom and get back to work.

MARCH 15, 2020

I've seen enough. This is not going away. It's not going to get better.

As my cab sprints down the FDR, my thumbs jump into maniacal action to post on my blog and social media: something the world wars did not have; maybe a double-edged sword? *But if I can convince even one person to stay home right now, it could save entire families and communities.*

I pull off my best impression of Paul Revere's ride. The pandemic is coming.

OOO

My PSA on COVID-19 testing: UNLESS it's a life- or limb-threatening emergency (e.g. you need oxygen or ventilatory support), DO NOT GO TO, OR GET ROUTINE COVID-19 TESTING IN AN ER!!!

What a week it's been—I've worked the past 7 days in 5 different ERs in NYC. Every site is figuring out their own version of PPE, testing capabilities, IT workflow, screening rules, approach guidelines. Outside field tents are going up, corridors are being sealed, surge capacity has begun. And since I can't ignore the elephant in the room, I've canceled all travel and will not commit to any trips until this madness blows over, hopefully by the summer.

As per diem (having the flexibility to pick up shifts whenever + wherever I choose and when there is the greatest need in NYC), I've ironically been working more shifts than I ever had expected to, now that so many of my ER colleagues are already calling out sick or being furloughed due to exposure to COVID-19: The writing is on the wall.

So while I do my part in this pandemic, I urge that you also do yours; we can still prevent a total collapse of our healthcare system if you can do one simple thing: unless it is a life- or limb-threatening emergency and/or you need oxygen or ventilatory support, STAY AWAY FROM OUR EMERGENCY ROOMS DURING THIS PANDEMIC. And PLEASE TELL EVERYONE that too.

"But what about testing? Isn't more testing better?"

Ah, but it doesn't work as well when you come to the ER—

Let's say you had no symptoms (or at best mild symptoms from something else), or had some other non-life- or limb-threatening concern, and you don't have COVID-19 but came to the ER anyway. Or let's say you came just for screening or a work clearance. So we then swab you and send out a test, but during the time you got on the subway, registered at triage, waited to be seen, or waited for discharge papers, you THEN unknowingly became exposed to someone else who actually has COVID-19—whether it was a sick patient shedding all that virus in the ER, a visitor, the guy sitting next to you on the bus, the work note you got that could act as a fomite, another worried well waiting for their test, or a health-care worker who was just exposed to COVID-19.

A few hours (or days) later, you then get the callback saying that your test for COVID-19 came back negative—when you actually caught it from riding public transportation or arriving at a high-volume area like the ER. Guess what? You're now falsely reassured with a false negative result, which means you're less likely to self-quarantine, and it ruins the whole point of screening in order to prevent unnecessary further community spread. Multiply that by an exponential factor, and now we're intubating your grandparents or your immunocompromised friends back-to-back next week. You might end up fine at the end of all this, but the person next to you—someone you love—might end up on life support.

So tell everyone you know to stay away from our ERs and let us take care of the ones who truly need our help. Wait for the home test kits or go to the drive-thru when they become available. At least at home or in your own private vehicle you can get screened AND minimize exposure to others and yourself.

Finally, us emergency physicians trained years for this, so please let us shoulder most of your worries; your panic makes it much harder for all of us. You can also make the world less shitty by not doing things like panic buying, gathering in crowds, and further spreading this virus to 80+ year olds and the immunocompromised who I then have to intubate next week. Please don't make us get to the point where we have to ration care by choosing who gets to live and who dies—there are fewer than 10,000 ventilators/breathing machines in NY State, and fewer than 160,000 in the country (to put that into perspective, health.ny.gov models expect 89,610 patients in NY state and over 740,000 in the country who would require ventilators/breathing machines during a severe 6-week outbreak on the level of the 1918 influenza pandemic). That scenario would be unforgiving.

Every little bit counts.

P.S. Don't forget to wash your hands with soap.

P.P.S. Don't be racist. And don't be a dick.

Now heading back to work for day 8 of 8!

Tonight at 1:30 a.m. EMS brings in a patient with severe shortness of breath. She can't complete sentences, even as she brokenly, in tears, tries to tell us she woke up unable to breathe. She and we know it is "the new virus." We hear crackles on her auscultation, but it's the chest X-ray that tells the tale: widespread ground glass opacities on both lungs indicative of viral pneumonia. Her oxygen saturation is 72 percent. But it's not just a number this time: She's also gasping, and it feels like we're headed for inevitable—and, this time, clinically viable—intubation. I advise her that this is the next step, but she cries harder, waving me off as though to stop an assault.

"But I don't"—she wheezes and grasps for a breath—"want to die."

She has likely heard the latest statistics from Europe and Asia: Only 14 percent of patients who are intubated survive. She does not want to be one of them. She does not want to be that number. She does not want to be *a* number.

I glance around. This ER is not large and for that reason is usually bypassed by ambulances. If we don't have anyone else like her arrive for the rest of the night, we could place her in our only isolation room on noninvasive ventilation known as BiPAP, where a Darth Vader–esque mask, instead of a breathing tube, pushes oxygen into a patient's lungs. This would reduce the work of breathing on her own and keep her awake, obviating the need for a medically induced coma. If our team is hypervigilant about maintaining our N95s and other PPE, we might be able to see her through the night without intubation until she can be moved to an open monitored bed upstairs.

She agrees, and after about an hour is breathing easier and out of acute distress. Another patient spared. And not for nothing, another ventilator spared.

MARCH 16, 2020

Only one unused N95 left in this ER at the start of my shift. I leave it for someone else. The old faithful I've brought with me looks filthy, so I spend a few minutes rubbing it down with a bleach wipe. *Better than nothing. I hope.*

The eye-watering reek of bleach and death now strapped to my face, I log on to a shared computer and see local headlines the previous shift's doctor had been reading:

Doctors Fear Bringing Coronavirus Home: 'I Am Sort of a Pariah in My Family'

Two Emergency Room Doctors Are in Critical Condition with Coronavirus

What fantastic motivational reading to start my shift. I wipe down my jacket and pants, too, for good measure. At least we have plenty of bleach wipes. For now.

By midnight, the board reads:

Discharge
Admit
Admit
Admit
Admit
Admit
Admit

Admit
Admit
Admit
Admit
Admit
AMA
Admit

It feels like there are more suspected COVID-19 patients here in the ER waiting for beds upstairs than there are actual beds upstairs. My Tetris nightmare has become reality sooner than my most pessimistic predictions. The one patient who just signed out against medical advice (AMA) probably sensed it too.

The hospital is full today. Please come back later.

MARCH 17, 2020

Bronx again. Tenth shift in a row. One-day-old face shield, three-day-old N95, seven-day-old pair of goggles. It could be worse. I'm sure it could be worse.

During my shift I take a sneak peek at news out of Italy. It's bad: stretchers crammed side by side down hallways, not much more crowded than what's piling up in this ER. In pictures their patients are all wearing oxygen helmets that make them look like they're part of a deep-sea diver convention at nap time. I'm informed later these are not FDA-cleared for use on our side of the ocean.

What I wouldn't give for a couple of those suckers, if not for patients, then for us . . .

MARCH 18, 2020

The past three mornings I've woken up thinking about the climactic ferry scene from *The Dark Knight*. My mind's ear conjures the razor blades on violin strings of Hans Zimmer and James Newton Howard's soundtrack. "We Are Tonight's Entertainment" screeches until I complete my personal inventory: Fever? No. Sore throat? No. Cough? No.

How long can my lucky streak last? And once it breaks, where do I go?

Ah, fear. Good to see you, old friend.

I recall once seeing a video of tiny me at the beach, outright panicked, kicking and screaming at my playful cousins who were trying to take off my shoes. That howling kid barely talked for the first six years of his life, so paralyzing was his anxiety. Heritable anxiety disorder from my mother's side? A childhood made insecure by an overbearing father? Both? Who knows. But by my late teens I was in a perpetual state of dread, not of being barefoot at the beach but of being abandoned and alone. My father's unexpected death, in some way, brought my deepest fear to life—and I survived. Soon after his funeral, I began to wonder: if death is one of the only things we still have in common and therefore something we must accept as unavoidable, then can we at least choose *how*, let alone *whether*, to run toward or be dragged into oblivion?

It was during his second memorial service that I felt more exhausted from all this thinking and the futile resistance against the inevitable. I could keep shedding frantic energy out in the universe, or I could be ready to receive. Perhaps I could get on a frequency with entropy by accepting I *am* it. Maybe only then would I be able to let go.

Despite my exhaustion, the internal questions yet persisted: *So what if I therefore choose to make friends with this fear of an unknown future, let it be a muse for living? What if, instead of hiding from fires, both real and imagined, I run toward and stay in the present flames?*

Like the irony of feeling more awake the more you try to sleep, the more I thought I knew what to do, the further away I felt from a resolution.

What feels like the half of my brain responsible for risk-taking then makes a suggestion: *if half the battle is showing up, then fake it till it manifests in you.* Once again, perhaps for the millionth time, I remind myself that reframing fear as a friend could, maybe, be the answer. *Yes, it's okay to be afraid. It's a fucking pandemic. This is your calling. Rise to it.*

And then, deep within the other half of my brain, the part that appears to be responsible for self-preservation, a cry retorts: *But you're also working as a per diem, so no one is making you work. If you sit this one out, you can choose to protect yourself and the loved ones around you.* I try to accommodate: so if half the battle is showing up, then could the other half be knowing when to stick it out and when to walk away?

Yeah! You already showed up. You got this far. You did your part.

A reply: *Ah, but are you going to run and hide, now that this fire has become an inferno? Is that the story you want?*

With dueling thoughts once again doling out more questions for every potential answer, I had finally had enough of this skull-side chitchat. Three deep breaths. *Excuse me, brain, can we let my feelings have a word in?*

As if they were patiently waiting for this debate to reach an impasse, they then make their contribution and I *feel* their answer: *I'd probably be way less afraid if I allowed myself the freedom to feel afraid.*

Ah, fear. Welcome back, old friend. Let's go.

~~~~

Hospitals Facing Coronavirus Are Running Out of Masks, Other Key Equipment

- *Some hospitals go the DIY route, while doctors and nurses clean and stretch out single-use gear. 'This is battlefield medicine.'*

UPDATED MARCH 18, 2020 1:47 PM ET

Hospitals across the U.S. are running out of the masks, gowns and other equipment they need to protect staff against the novel coronavirus as they struggle to take care of patients, say hospital officials, doctors and others in the industry.

The Pentagon stepped into the breach by offering on Tuesday to supply up to five million respirator masks, as health-care officials and workers say the situation is dire.

Administrators at the Renton, Wash., headquarters of the Providence health system are in conference rooms assembling makeshift face shields from vinyl, elastic and two-sided tape because supplies are drying up. Nurses from Brigham and Women's Hospital in Boston, preparing for a potential shortage, have pleaded with friends on Facebook for any goggles and other gear they might have lying around.

"I'm reusing my mask from yesterday," said Calvin Sun, an emergency-room doctor in New York City. "We really have no choice."[1]

10 YEARS AGO

~~~~~~~~~

Winter 2010: Birth of the Monsoon

Echoes of M83's "Highway of Endless Dreams" roll on in my slumber, leaving me no choice but to awake into the black. If the clock is to be believed, it's 3:00 a.m. A glance around tells me I'm not home, so I comb through what's left of my short-term memory: *Cairo*.

Five days ago, I made a bet with two friends that I would join them on a last-minute trip to Egypt if, and only if, I could find an equally last-minute round-trip flight for less than . . . let's say . . . $800—a random number I had used to signify a relatively low price, since the current average at the time was about two grand. Although I mostly wasn't serious when I told them that, I also had realized my annual paid vacation days were about to expire and I honestly didn't want them to go to waste. Plus, finding my father's good camera lenses had me dreaming about photographing the world. I joked, therefore, that if I found an absurdly cheap ticket by the time they left for their planned trip, I would meet them in Cairo.

I had never traveled on my own volition internationally. Hell, I'd barely been outside New York City by myself. But when I checked prices a few hours after my toss-off bet, I was shocked to see $650 roundtrip on the screen. *Damn. Is the universe testing me?* Before I knew it I was on a plane to Amman, Jordan, for a connection to Cairo. I reasoned that I would rather be a man of my word and $650 poorer, than to begin making a habit of not following through on my promises.

Half the battle is showing up.

Lying here in a kind of darkness my eyes don't know how to cope with, I recall my recent transatlantic flight that I had just taken to Amman. Flight attendants had announced someone was suffering from what appeared to be a heart attack. If there were no medical personnel on board, the pilot would have to turn the plane around. I had pushed the call button. Does two years of volunteering as a patient advocate and EKG technician "red shirt" in Bellevue Hospital Center's emergency room count? Better than nothing. Two other passengers, retired nurses, also offered assistance. The man's eyes were rolled back, he was unresponsive, and he seemed to be semiconscious. We gave him aspirin and asked for the onboard defibrillator, but before we could use it, he awakened. He couldn't remember anything other than having complained of chest pain, but assured us he was feeling better.

Whether it was low blood sugar, a seizure, a vasovagal response, or an actual cardiopulmonary event, he would stay awake the rest of the flight. I had offered to sit next to him and measure his pulse and blood pressure every half hour, keeping myself awake with free caffeinated beverages and two full repeated viewings of *He's Just Not That into You*. He barely acknowledged me with a moment of brief eye contact and a half-smile. I don't need much.

Now, here on this cotton mattress at what feels to my inner New Yorker like 9:00 p.m. but, according to the clock, is the future, I think, *Maybe being a doctor wouldn't be so bad. I might be good at it. I might . . . like it?* A sense of purpose suddenly fills me.

Landing in Cairo, I'd paid for the visa on arrival and met my friends, one of whom had already gotten a new tattoo to commemorate the trip. After a light dinner together, they had dropped me off at a hostel with instructions to meet them "behind the Oberoi Hotel in Giza at 4:00 a.m.," as if I knew what any of those words mean.

I gather my things and sneak into the shadow of the city, and by some miracle hail a lonely cab from Tahrir Square to the Oberoi Hotel twenty minutes away. I find my friends around the back, and not far away is the group of Bedouins, a predominantly desert-dwelling Arabian ethnic group who live mainly off-grid, who will guide us to the pyramids. Inhibitions blitzed by jet lag and the near delirium of surreality, I indicate that I want to ride one of their horses rather than climb into a camel howdah. Asked if I've ridden before, I lie: "Of course!" *Fear is my friend. Fear is my friend. Fear is . . .*

With the sound of a whip cracking cold desert air, my life changes forever. The horse races and so does my heart, and I hold on to both for dear life. My mount gallops as if desperate to outrun his past or his fate, and the ring of his hooves on pavement gives way to a soft pulse on rustling sand. I'm not in New York anymore. I breathe and fly through the Sahara in utter darkness. Terror and exhilaration inform me I am still alive. Pulses and breaths.

Figures are silhouetted by a fire in the distance, and behind me the muezzins begin the morning *adhan*, calling the faithful to prayer. We will watch the sun come up over the Great Pyramids at the Bedouin camp, smoking shisha, sipping hot tea, and exchanging smiles of shared appreciation.

Best bet I ever lost.

• • •

Days later, I sit alone in a Cairo train station. It's getting dark and I have no plan. No laptop, no cell phone, no internet access, no local friend to call even if I could figure out the pay phone. A thick fog of humanity drifts to and fro, without a care for me. And I am but a droplet in this fog, unnoticed.

I can't make sense of this contradictory swirl of emotions. I remain formless, barely a blip on the radar of existence, yet because of that also liberated. I'm unreachable. I know no one. No one knows me. I'm not about to run into an acquaintance by happenstance. I can't even understand the ubiquitous ads telling me what to buy and do. Everything except "I" is a blank to me. I can commune only with myself.

I am truly free.

It is thrilling. It is awful.

I am in a *dérive*.

I like this. I hate this. I like this more than I hate this.

Having freed myself of structure, routine, and familiarity for a time, I'm now engulfed in, entrapped by, bottomless fear. It does not feel like a friend. *It never does.* Alone on a bench in Cairo, I feel immobilized. Perhaps by doing absolutely nothing I can regain some sense of security. Like a deer in the headlights, I'm frozen in my tracks. Complete inaction is my only hope of survival. From bench to beach, I'm back being tiny me, screaming and kicking as my cousins playfully take off my shoes.

When the idea of staying put and sleeping on this bench presents itself as a viable, even appealing, option, I force myself to walk a step toward the present flames—then another step before another, as I make it to the counter and buy a one-way ticket for Alexandria. Four or five hours later, I force myself to disembark from the train.

Then I force myself to leave Alexandria station. Each struggle adds to a list of things to do but also cuts into my bandwidth.

I walk, stop, turn around, stop again, turn around again, walk a few more paces, and turn again without any idea where I'm going. I cross a bridge, go down some stairs and under another bridge, and realize the futility of using the station as a landmark to orient myself. I am lost. I don't yet know how to read maps, so I bite the bullet and get a cab to the Corniche, Alexandria's waterfront, where I might find a hotel. Three hours later and knocking on plenty of doors, I finally fall into an unfamiliar bed. (Years later I'm still not entirely sure how I stumbled onto that cheap and spartan guesthouse, and I'm still thankful that I did.)

I wake the next morning with mosquito bites and a fever—only it's not, I realize, a real fever but just more fear, leaving me sweaty and ill at ease. I don't want to leave this guesthouse. I will stay here and do absolutely nothing. Complete inaction and lack of purpose may be my only hope of survival.

I sit in the living room that doubles as a guest lobby for an hour, at once fidgeting and inert, before I can force myself to at least peek outside. Then a step outside. I reason that survival is one thing, but total paralysis from fear could be a worst fate. *Time to go, old friend. Let's find a fire and run toward it.*

Once I'm through the door, retreating isn't an option: The house owners lock up from the inside each day.

I remain grateful, these many years later, to those inhospitable hosts. They didn't baby me; they were the best hosts I could ever ask for.

With no other choice, I go where the wind blows on my back. Exploring Alexandria, Egypt, on my own, wandering the streets of a foreign country alone and without a plan, the travel bug bites hard, latches on, and burrows deep: *Resfeber.* The fever is upon me.

This would mark my first time traveling alone and endeavoring to see everything a new place has to offer in a short amount of time, all without having a clue what the next step will look like. My first time consciously embracing the comfort of being uncomfortable when it comes to new experiences and travel. Travel the impossible, even. Within months many of my fellow companions would later tease the way I travel and call this "monsooning." While I had never been one for labels, this exception would stick. And I've always been one for exceptions. Besides, I like it when it rains.

Because the next time I would experience this feeling again would be less than half a year later, when I'm caught under an unexpected summer monsoonal cloudburst in South Asia. I'm also caught smiling when this happens.

Whoever said only sunshine brought happiness has never danced in the rain.

And then it disappears as quickly as it had come.

Storms shall always come and pass: It's what and how we *do* when one arrives that matters. My new oath and code.

Monsooning is born.

DYSPNEA

≈≈≈≈≈≈

March 19–29, 2020

n. (disp·né·uh) difficult or labored
breathing; shortness of breath.

MARCH 19, 2020

It feels as if the dwellers in the ivory towers of the Centers for Disease Control have just been born into the pandemic as they offer some guidance to us frontline healthcare providers today:

When No Facemasks Are Available, Options Include

HCP use of homemade masks: In settings where facemasks are not available, HCP [healthcare personnel] might use homemade masks (e.g., bandana, scarf) for care of patients with COVID-19 as a last resort. However, homemade masks are not considered PPE, since their capability to protect HCP is unknown. Caution should be exercised when considering this option. Homemade masks should ideally be used in combination with a face shield that covers the entire front (that extends to the chin or below) and side of the face.[1]

That's cute, CDC. We don't even have proper masks—which you even acknowledged by suggesting scarves and bandanas. So what makes you think, just three sentences later in your statement, that we have fancy face shields at the very same healthcare facilities that don't even supply proper masks??

Exclude HCP at higher risk for severe illness from COVID-19 from contact with known or suspected COVID-19 patients: During severe resource limitations, consider excluding HCP who may be at higher risk for severe illness from COVID-19, such as those of older age, those with chronic medical conditions, or those who may be pregnant, from caring for patients with confirmed or suspected COVID-19 patients.[2]

I don't want the most vulnerable of my colleagues to be exposed, but I also don't want to be cannon fodder and shoulder all the risk. *Hello, rock. Oh, hi there to you, too, hard place.*

Designate convalescent HCP for provision of care to known or suspected COVID-19 patients: It may be possible to designate HCP who have clinically recovered from COVID-19 to preferentially provide care for additional patients with COVID-19. Individuals who have recovered from COVID-19 infection may have developed some protective immunity, but this has not yet been confirmed.[3]

To me this also reads as: "Congratulations on getting shot, falling off a cliff, and surviving! Now get back in there."

Current projections I've seen have the NYC surge peaking around May 1, with between 18,600 and 37,000 ICU beds needed by that time. We currently have in the ballpark of 3,000; all but about 500 already taken. In other words, according to my back-of-the-envelope math, we have somewhere between 13 percent (at best) and 7 percent (at worst) of the beds we'll need when it's Grandma's turn to go on life support.

I cross the Manhattan Bridge into Brooklyn for shift twelve of twelve in a row and learn a field tent with negative pressure will be up and running here by tomorrow morning. Christmas has come early this year! *While I have you on the line, Santa, I'd like a bunny suit and full PPE, please. Why the hell not: I'll take a PAPR while you're at it.*

I reach into my bag and come up with two disreputable-looking N95s. I honestly had no idea how many were in there, and now I'm not sure which one is fresher, relatively speaking. One is three days old, the other is four, maybe five. A nurse in the staff room witnesses my dilemma from afar and smuggles me a brand-spanking-new N95 out of pity. I want to give her a hug, but that may not be a good idea these days. Even attempting physical signs of gratitude have now become collateral damage of the pandemic.

I verbally thank her and look at her donation. *How can I extend this one's shelf life?* I decide I'll cover the precious filtered mask with a paper surgical mask *plus* a scarf I had bought as a souvenir last year monsooning on the island of Socotra (after all, since the CDC now recommends that healthcare providers use bandanas as PPE, I don't feel as alone in my inadequate efforts to stay alive). With twenty patients waiting to be seen, all suffering from shortness of breath, I feel like I'm running naked into a Category 5 hurricane.

At some point during the whirlwind morning, I get a text from an ER nurse I worked with in the Bronx:

> Using half of a padded bra for face mask :-(

Then another from her a couple of hours later:

> A couple other people are using period pads.

A local nurse taps me on the shoulder. "We literally only have ten swabs left," he says. "We need to save COVID testing for people you're admitting to the hospital so we know where to cohort them upstairs."

"But even the new in-house tests take two to three days to get back a result," I object. I'm met with a shrug. "So they're going to stay downstairs with us for forty-eight to seventy-two hours before they can get a bed upstairs? What about new patients, where are they supposed to go? Philadelphia?"

"Yup, it's a problem," he replies. "Can't do anything about it. Admin thinks they're better downstairs with us than upstairs with them."

"We're goners," I groan, "the walking dead."

When I get home, I spray down all three N95s with Lysol. I have no idea if this is a good idea.

~~~~

U.S. Hospitals Are Wildly Unprepared to Deal with How Bad the Coronavirus Pandemic Could Get

MARCH 19, 2020, 3:00 P.M.

For the last ten days, Dr. Calvin D. Sun has been working in emergency rooms throughout New York City and treating patients with COVID-19, the disease caused by the coronavirus. The 33-year-old physician specializes in emergency medicine, and he's been filling in when hospitals have a shortage of doctors.

Last week, he said ERs were rationing tests. "Next week the triage might be different: We might be rationing care," he said. "Everyone could be intubated, the hospitals might be full, the ICUs are full, we don't have enough ventilators."

Physicians and nurses across the country have already seen an overwhelming number of patients. More than 2,300 new cases of COVID-19 were confirmed on Wednesday alone, bringing the national total up to 10,442. And 150 people have died. With a shortage of beds, intensive care units, respirators, doctors, or nurses, the country's hospitals will soon be overwhelmed as those patients' symptoms worsen.[4]

MARCH 20, 2020

Can't shake off the stranglehold COVID has on me even on my first day off since getting back from Angola: This pandemic is so rude.

My friend Sheryl shows up at my door around noon and asks if she can come in for a minute. Turns out, my prayers yesterday have been answered and she's Santa's little helper: She's brought unused N95s, just for me. My N95 clock resets again. Out of habit of formality from a time before a pandemic, I ask out of reflex if she wants to come inside for a glass of water or to have lunch. She pauses to consider the changed circumstances of these times.

"You're dangerous, gotta go," she says, and leaves as quickly as she came. *Rude. At least stay for me to say thank you!*

A few hours later, my best friend from high school, Lei, and his wife, Maria, bike over from Flushing, Queens, to deliver some N95s they'd found in storage. They keep their distance but observe my body language. "Man, you look shell-shocked." *Rude.* I want to give them a hug anyway. They politely decline.

I then turn on the news and see New York mayor Bill de Blasio predicting hospitals will run out of "certain supplies" in two to three weeks. *Rude. Try two to three weeks ago, Mr. Mayor.*

Another hour goes by and I get a text from a co-worker to a link for an *LA Times* story from February 25 with the headline "Doctors and Nurses Fighting Coronavirus in China Die of Both Infection and Fatigue."[5] *Rude.* I initially don't click through. *Thanks, but no thanks.*

And then I click anyway, which then leads me to another article: Apparently LA County is advising doctors to give up testing unless a positive result would change how a patient would be treated.[6] This merely makes official and puts in writing what has been our default all along—the nationwide test shortage means we've had to be strategic about whom we test from day one: For example, is a patient in such bad shape that they need to be admitted to the hospital? If yes, we'll test them to confirm *where* they should be moved to upstairs. If no, a positive or negative test won't change our medical advice: *Stay home.* Assume the worst out of an abundance of caution for yourself and your loved ones. Save a test. Isolate. Hydrate. Rest. Come back if you experience shortness of breath. Otherwise until we have a surplus of tests, let me say it louder for the kids in the back: *Stay. Home.*

Governor Cuomo's office issues this cheery recruitment letter, which feels one step short of a draft card (see next page).

MARCH 21, 2020

Another text from the battlefield, this one bizarrely, refreshingly upbeat:

> Experimented this morning and found you can put surgical masks AND 3M N95s in the microwave and it's safe (with the thin metal too)! Two min on high removes 99% of living organisms from sponges and clothes, so same with masks. You may laugh but to me this means we can 'microwave sterilize' our N95s throughout the day to reuse. Crazier ideas have worked for other desperate situations?

Desperate, indeed. Doesn't sound right either; I'll make sure to keep my microwaves only for things I can eat, thank you.

STATE OF NEW YORK
EXECUTIVE CHAMBER
ALBANY 12224

ANDREW M. CUOMO
GOVERNOR

March 20, 2020

Dear Health Professional:

In the event that the novel coronavirus crisis worsens, we need the help of additional qualified health professionals and related professionals to supplement our hospital capacity on a temporary basis to treat seriously ill coronavirus patients including those that may need to be intubated.

If you are available, we need the following information immediately:

- Your specific qualifications and experience
- Date of last certification and license
- Last date of practice
- Role in last practice
- Contact information including location
- Current age
- Would you be willing to work in other parts of New York State?
- Describe your interest and ability to be able to provide your services to treat patients if the need should arise in the future.

Please provide these responses within 36 hours using this survey: www.health.ny.gov/assistance. If you have any questions please contact workforce@exec.ny.gov. Your immediate attention is necessary and appreciated.

With your help, New York State is working to protect our residents and strengthen our public health system to deal. We appreciate your commitment to the health and safety of all New Yorkers and look forward to building on our partnership.

Michael Dowling, President & CEO of Northwell Health, and Kenneth Raske, President, Greater New York Hospital Association, are leading this "surge project" for me and I hope you cooperate. It is as important an issue as we have ever seen.

Sincerely,

ANDREW M. CUOMO

. . .

On a non-pandemic morning at the top of a typical shift, I can expect four to six patients waiting to be seen in this single-coverage unit, where I am the one and only ER attending. Right now there are twenty-four patients, and twenty-one of them have symptoms—cough, respiratory distress, fever, headache, syncope (passing out), flu-like symptoms—all consistent with a possible coronavirus infection. The other three, an elderly woman with no family who has been falling at home more often recently, a guy with a laceration that requires stitches, and someone with acute abdominal pain, have now been exposed to COVID-19 and so will need to quarantine if we get them out of here. And wait, don't forget about me and my staff who came to work.

Half the battle has been showing up.

We will quickly admit the poor geriatric woman because she lives alone and can risk falling again at home. However, we also take pause at her multiple COVID risk factors with her age and a medical history including chronic obstructive pulmonary disorder. So while I hate that we have to send her upstairs to be exposed to an even bigger viral load, what else can we do? Send her home without medical support to very possibly die alone? Soon the life-and-death dilemma of which option is better hits her as well:

"Oh Lord, what should I do?" She cries out loud, mimicking our thoughts. I feel as if other patients in the emergency room also all seem to acknowledge this with a nod in their collective predicament.

This sucks: It's one thing to swear to "do no harm," and it's another when you realize either scenario we choose for her can equally lead to harm. When even longstanding oaths cannot provide us a clear solution, this becomes moral injury.

People are now terrified, for good reason, but some are even now taking it out on me and my staff. At some point today each of us has been yelled or cursed at (or both) by an agitated patient.

I get you're terrified. I get you're human. We're also terrified. We're also human. This is how your friendly neighborhood health-care worker might lose it.

I get another text, this time from another nurse I've worked with in a Bronx emergency department:

> We are all fucked. Nurses are getting sick left and right. What happens when all [our] ICU and ED RNs are out sick? You can't have medical/surgical nurses caring for vents or practicing ED medicine without at least some training. Why can't we start training now before it's too late? And why can't we get PPE so we DON'T GET SICK in the first place??

"Calvin, I'm afraid." I turn my attention to one of the nurses. His eyes are brimming. For the first time ever—six years in ERs, triaging mass casualty events, learning to ration care in parts of the world with limited resources—I take a break on shift for a good cry. Several other nurses join us in the breakroom for tearful catharsis, releasing a little bit of the pressure we're all cooking in.

I step out a few minutes later and approach the charge nurse and the nurse supervisor to say, "If this keeps up, things are going to fall apart. Bad things are going to happen."

"I'm scared too," says the charge nurse. She looks to the nurse supervisor, who picks up the phone to call our department chair. The reply: *"I understand but there's just not enough staff today. We don't have enough providers."*

Powerless to do anything else but convey concerns and sound alarms, I put my mask and goggles back on and return to my trenches of fire and brimstone.

This is fine. This is awful.

. . .

My phone is now blowing up with requests to cover other doctors' shifts.

> Want my Monday 1:30–11:30?

> *Already working Monday.*

> No worries, crazy time for nyc.

> *Yeah, tomorrow will be my 12th shift out of 15 days.*

> Omg take a breather.

> I've had fevers for 48 hrs.

> *Please take care of yourself!*

> I'm the 2nd attending to get sick.

> *I'm probably right behind you.*

~~~~~

> We've got to get them to separate resp patients. 100% this is why we're getting sick. This is a death sentence. Cardiologist colleague (51) is critically ill with the virus, cardiologist fellow who runs marathons (32) also very sick. It's not just the young.

> My symptoms are minor but what if I give it to my 50+ physician's assistant or to my patients?

> Older NYU ER physician just coded.

> One of our infectious disease docs is in the ICU.

I used to get one text every three or four days to cover for sick colleagues; now it's three or four texts each day. Every healthcare worker in New York now knows a colleague who is intubated, in critical condition, on life support.

While I'm immensely grateful that people are donating masks to us, what we have always needed upon the discovery of any pathogen with pandemic potential are full-body Tyvek bunny suits with face shields or PAPRs. Masks lower the risk of infection, but they are dimmer switches to an exposure, not circuit breakers. Plus, patients and visiting family members have been caught stealing our masks and supplies to the point where we now have to lock them all away (making them even harder for us to access when we need them immediately).

We are running out of masks.

We are running out of beds.

We are running out of medicine.

We are running out of vents.

We are running out of staff.

We are running out of time.

MARCH 22, 2020

Last night I started anonymizing and posting the texts and messages I've received from healthcare workers across the city in response to my stories on social media. This morning there are dozens more replies from doctors, nurses, administrators, and other healthcare providers I don't know from around the country. If I can't do anything in my present physical space, I'm going to keep sharing anonymously (or not, if they request to be named) in my social medial spaces until my hands fall off. Seems like the least I can do to help my colleagues feel heard. But who knows if anyone is listening?

New York City's lockdown officially begins at 8:00 p.m. today. I predict this will actually ramp *up* the number of people seeking hospital treatment. Guess I'll find out firsthand during my ten-hour shift that starts at 4:00 p.m.

The first problem I find this afternoon is no surgical caps and gowns. They've run out. I leave on the ski jacket and beanie I brought as a precaution and get to work, just so there's a layer to take off when I'm done—but I'm already sweating. Not a fever. Just too many clothes.

Around 5:00 we run out of bleach wipes, which I discover when I go to wipe down my stethoscope between patients. *What the fuck. What's next, toilet paper?*

An anesthesiologist and friend from medical school messages at 6:30:

> The hospital I'm in is a cesspool. Took a shift here, it's overwhelmed. What if this is just the beginning? Hang in there, Calvin.

Another reports:

> Doc husband says people are using garbage bags as gowns.

One hospital's trash has literally become another one's treasure.

. . .

At 8:00 the lockdown goes into effect, and a few of us step outside for some fresh air and a look around. There are EMS stretchers end to end down the ramp and ambulances lined up around the block waiting to offload their human cargo. Kateryna, a nurse standing next to me, quips, "Let the war begin."

By 9:00 the electronic medical record (EMR) board is exploding with new registrations. Desk staff tell me the average wait time from ambulance to triage is now five hours. *Holy shit, five hours?* I imagine calling 911 for an emergency, thinking I'll get immediate care, only to wait five hours in subfreezing temperatures for someone to check me in.

After reading my social media update on the bleach wipes situation, another nurse friend messages:

> We're throwing paper towels in empty bleach wipe containers to soak up the last of the juices.

Helpful. I push this stop-gap solution out to my social media. But what if we run out of paper towels too? Use the napkins from our food deliveries?

Other providers send pictures from their neck of the woods. One shows the shape of a person wearing a plastic bag with SOILED LINEN, ROPA SUCIO printed upside down, captioned, "Yes, that is our ER attending wearing a laundry bag to treat COVID patients."

Another personal text at around 1:00 in the morning:

> Some hospitals telling staff not to use PPE. Sonographer told by administration to screen everyone coming in but DON'T wear PPE because it will scare people.

Can that be true? I push it out to whoever's listening on social media and ask if anyone else is seeing something similar. Replies through the wee hours continue to blow up my phone:

> This literally happened to me last week when I was screening families! Administrators thought I was crazy for wanting to wear a mask and basically guilted me into NOT wearing it cuz we have low supply. I kept 6 feet away from everyone, then the same admins had masks and goggles the next day lol.

> Family friend got fired for wearing a mask at her hospital. Fucked up.

> Literally got yelled out in front of everyone for wearing N95 in room 3 days ago.

> This is happening at my mom's hospital in Michigan, a nurse was fired for wearing a mask :(

In hospitals around the country, administrators are telling frontline healthcare workers to take off their PPE because it scares people. It "doesn't look good." *This pandemic doesn't look good. Is anyone on our side?*

This isn't war. Feels more like murder, a one-sided slaughter, like that opening scene from *Enemy at the Gates* where panicked soldiers get shot by their own very side for retreating.

Later I'll catch sight of a *Forbes* magazine headline from today:

Doctors Don't Perform Well When They Are Afraid

MARCH 22, 2020, 09:00 A.M.[7]

No shit. In other news, water is wet.

MARCH 23, 2020

Thousands more followers on social media today for my updates. I've gone "viral." Although the irony of that adjective now sickens me considering the circumstances, I feel determined to keep sharing stories of my fellow healthcare providers. Maybe someone *is* listening.

Friend from med school texts:

> At this point as an asthmatic I almost WANT to get it as long as I'm going to get over it. Just so I can stop living with the stress of getting it.

I smell the stink of my own breath in my N95 and almost don't catch myself before I take it off for a breather. Habits. Who knows if I already unknowingly sucked the virus in today? Even muscle memory is killing us along with everything else. Who would've guessed how many times a day we actually touch our faces?

I overhear someone ask, "Where's so-and-so?" and the inevitable answer, "They got COVID."

"Oh," the first voice responds. "That's why there's so many new faces."

This morning's vibe is less frantic, but also less hopeful, than yesterday's. Some of us are looking as if we've embraced some measure of acceptance. Or despair. Masks off. Drier tears. Thousand-yard stares. Which stage of grief are we at now? Is this depression or acceptance? Other than a slight shade of shadow gray, I can't tell the difference.

I step outside, take off my mask, and catch sight of my reflection in the hospital's windows. I've got what look like bad tattoos along my nasal bridge and folds. The top layer of skin seems to be breaking down and turning to scar tissue. I remember seeing pictures in January of healthcare workers from Wuhan and anticipated when it would be our turn to share their scars; the day has arrived earlier than we expected.

By 11:00 a.m. we're delivering a baby in the resuscitation room when I hear a middle-aged patient, obviously not in respiratory distress, screaming outside: "Where is everyone?!"

The closest nurse becomes collateral damage and pleads with her, "Ma'am, everyone is busy trying to help someone else who's having an emergency."

Someone else chimes in, "A patient is having a baby!"

The offending patient goes off: "Who the fuck asked you? She's having a baby? Well, I don't fucking care if she's having a baby! What the fuck am I doing in the ER if nobody is coming to help me? Nobody is helping *me*!"

The nurse tries one more time, "Ma'am . . ."

"FUCK YOU. I want a test!"

She continues to scream, but everyone else is too tired or shell-shocked to respond with anything but an under-the-breath "Jesus take the wheel."

I debate whether to step out and help, but my nurse supervisor stops and grounds me. "Baby first. That screaming lady called 911 so she could skip the line and get a COVID test. No symptoms, normal vitals."

Three minutes later there's a new, healthy baby in the world (and what a world it is), and I confront the source of the screams. The continuous volley of *fuck you*s exhausts all her strikes, so the nurse supervisor, a security guard, and I escort the asymptomatic screamer out of the ER and into a taxi, wishing her the best of luck.

I glance at the EMR on the way back in and see we have a new column for testing status:

Positive
Negative
Positive
Positive
Positive
Negative

Negative

Positive

Positive

Positive

Positive

Positive

Positive

Positive

Positive

Positive

Positive

Positive

Positive

Positive

Negative

Positive

Positive

Positive

Positive

Positive

The goal for kicking the screamer out was to stop the abuse of staff and patients in my ER, but I've also probably saved her life by minimizing her exposure to the virus. The irony. *And you're welcome.*

Still more messages from battlefields around the country:

> No protective clothing at all. It's CRAZY how horrible the US is in taking care of healthcare workers. My sister said a nurse in her neuro ICU tested positive but they won't test any of the doctors who had contact with her.

> Family friend who's a nurse in NJ told not to bring her own mask since other nurses don't have them and it scares patients. Risk her health or lose her job?? That's the choice.

It now occurs to me that I'm either about to reframe, justify, or realize another major upside to my choice not to sign a full-time hospital contract but rather stay a per diem freelancer: There's no "boss" or hospital administrator who has the leverage of job security over me to tell me what to wear, what to do, or what to say on the media. I would learn that because of the perception of my *choosing* to show up to this understaffed Chernobyl, they are currently receiving me with open arms. I wonder what it would be like to have little choice and be forced to work under all their rules? I hate that for my colleagues. Or what if I'm deluding myself and maybe my own point of burnout and moral injury is just right around the corner, only a bit more delayed by this false sense of autonomy? Time will tell.

The ER's red phone for imminent emergency notifications rings. Stroke? Cardiac arrest? Trauma? The desk clerk answers it, then immediately hangs up.

"What was that?" I ask.

"Someone just called the emergency room to ask if we have Wi-Fi. I'm done."

Another exhausted voice quips, "Should've told him we have Wi-Fi with a side of COVID."

• • •

I return home at 6:00 p.m., and it feels like another Christmas morning. Ten boxes of N95s, four of surgical masks, two face shields, and two pairs of shoe covers on my doorstep: all dropped off by my older brother, Linus, travel buddies Mihaela (who came by for a few seconds without saying a word in the middle of what appears to be a random monsoon) and Anderson (who shipped them from Texas), childhood friend Karen, and friends Donald, Everett, Tudor, Michelle, Lindsay, and Ana. *I am saved.*

I post my thanks and tag them all:

O O O

At every shift from now on, I will give away as many as I can so your donations save as many lives as possible. Thank you.

My eye catches the pink filters of a different type of mask: a P100. The MVP goes to Linus, who has smuggled one of these from his lab. "P" means the filter is even oil resistant unlike the "N" filters on N95s, and "100" means it filters out particles as small as 0.3 microns 99.7 percent of the time, compared to the 95 percent of an N95. I now have PPE just one step below a PAPR, the mythical "helmet astronaut thing from a movie released in 1995" that no one seems able to track down still.

I know the size of a SARS-CoV-2 virus is smaller than 0.3 microns, but if it spreads by droplets—many of which are larger than 0.3 microns—I'll take this P100 with a side of celebration. Having *any* PPE to share is vastly preferable to the shit I was swimming upstream in last week. Small wins now are still wins.

The next gift to unwrap is a spray bottle of premixed 70 percent isopropyl alcohol. Last time I used one of these was working in a college lab culturing and pipetting cells. *Sweet.* I have the power to spray down this dirty, dirty world.

The biggest box is also from my brother's lab, and it's a gift that will keep on giving: a head-to-toe protective suit, a "bunny suit," with a nifty Tyvek sticker and everything. I suit up just to see how it fits, feeling like a kid on Halloween. No more garbage bags. Sure, bunny suits, like N95s, are designed for a single patient interaction. But you can bet I'll be in this sucker each and every shift going forward.

Both grateful and frustrated, I remark online that we're desperate for the 95 percent protection of N95s when what we really need is the nearly 100 percent protection of P100s and PAPRs. A fellow doctor responds:

> ○ ○ ○
>
> I said this out loud [about PAPRs] in the SICU last week and
> the admin response was, shhh, yeah, um, N95's all we've
> got though, so . . . even when we're informed, we're fucked.

MARCH 24, 2020

Ten in the morning in a South Bronx ER. The schedule puts
me in the COVID-only area for the next twelve hours. This
unit is big enough to separate non-COVID-emergent cases
from the larger population of viral patients. What should be
the norm for hospital protocol feels like an absolute luxury.

I've got a bulging grocery bag at my side and I hold it up
in the staff room: "Who needs N95s?"

Hands everywhere. They go like hotcakes. Early holiday
cheer for everyone.

I don my bunny suit and P100, and for once feel ready to
take on the day. What an unfamiliar feeling.

Then I get a text from my brother, quoting a study that's
just been released:

> "Data from @StanfordEng Professors and
> @yicustandford and Steven Chu show #N95masks can
> be decontaminated [sic] without decreasing filtration
> efficiency using 70C heat for 30 min. **Alcohol and
> bleach should not be used.**

"... Conclusions: **Do NOT use alcohol and chlorine-based disinfection methods.** These will remove the static charge in the microfibers in the N95 facial masks, reducing filtration efficiency. In addition, chlorine also retains gas after de-contamination and these fumes may be harmful."

My heart skips a beat: We've been doing it wrong for two weeks. The cough and fever will hit me any minute now. I swallow again to check for a sore throat and decide to look it up for myself to confirm or cross-reference. *Maybe the jury is still out. If not, we've been fucking ourselves over by "decontaminating" our N95s to reuse.*

I find a video of a woman filling up an N95 mask with water, which seems to hold up within the mask. Another woman walks over with what appears to be a bottle of alcohol and sprays the mask once, and water pours through the mask like a faucet. *Is this fake? Another TikTok challenge? This is a horror movie.* I see my spray bottle of 70 percent isopropyl alcohol sitting next to the bag of N95s and move them away from each other as if they were at a parochial middle school dance, to avoid the unlikely risk of cross-contamination if they get too close. Or as if they could give COVID-19 to each other.

I'll keep spraying down my work station, but you can bet I'll keep the masks out of the way from now on. *So how come I don't have symptoms yet?*

MARCH 25, 2020

Done at 11:00 p.m. last night; shift 14 since March 8 starts in twenty-six minutes. Manhattan turns into Queens under the indigo ink sky of a predawn morning. I'm headed to another new-to-me ER in need of pandemic staffing coverage. Hopefully I spend more time with patients than figuring out an unfamiliar electronic medical record system.

My bag of N95s is empty minutes after I arrive. I recall those innocent days not too long ago when new staff would bring a box of adult-onset diabetes such as donuts or pizza to win over staff on a new shift. *Those were the days.*

"RAPID RESPONSE TEAM TO ROOM 605," a detached voice yells over the intercom. If a patient's heart or breathing stops, we say they're "coding." On an average day in an average hospital, a "code" happens once every few hours for a patient experiencing cardiac or respiratory arrest who needs immediate lifesaving maneuvers and resuscitation. The past three days, in three different NYC hospitals, I've heard this announcement roughly once an hour. People are losing their pulses and breaths literally left and right.

By today's end, the news anchors will announce that 220 Americans have died from COVID. And I will have personally been present for 4.5 percent of that number.

A flood of updates from colleagues I trust around the city continue to stream in on social media, and when I get a minute I push them out to those following my updates, the number of which continues to grow. My colleagues are desperate to share what's happening to them; when they learn that other colleagues are reporting a similar problem elsewhere, they begin a healing process recognizing how they're not alone in their silos and institutions.

You are not alone.

I now hear that at multiple hospitals, regular medical or surgical floors are being converted into intensive care unit (ICU) overflow. Short of the morgue, ICU is as sick as you can get. A typical ICU in a large hospital has staffing and resources to care for eight to ten patients at a time. Today one such hospital that I've worked in has over fifty critically ill patients. This can only mean extremely sick people receiving substandard care from undersupported, exhausted staff who were already stretched way too thin even before this pandemic.

Staffing has always been a massive problem everywhere, but it looks different from hospital to hospital because each administration sets its own policies. Some are responding to the sudden drop in revenue from canceled elective surgeries by furloughing regular employees. Some are automatically quarantining entire teams after a single positive case without knowing how to quickly and adequately replace them. Internal policies are all over the place as everyone tries to cope with the unthinkable.

As our frontline numbers thin, other specialties are sending down their nurse practitioners and PAs to help manage ER surge capacity. That means people who specialize in gastroenterology or oral surgery are receiving a crash course in the specialty of emergency medicine.

I hear that some ERs are intubating ten to twelve patients per day. I've instructed my own staff wherever I work a shift that we'll intubate only if we have no other choice, but I get reports from other doctors who are using intubation as a prophylactic against worsening outcomes, even if it may cause more harm than good. None of us still truly knows which approach is right, clinically speaking. I guess for many they will lean on the fifth verse of the modern Hippocratic Oath —swearing there is no shame when one admits "I know not"—when it clashes with the agony over *primum non nocere*, "first do no harm." Another moral injury to add to the list.

There are only one or two ventilators left in some hospitals, including the one I'm in right now. I wonder what will happen when a third patient needing intubation comes in? Some hospitals are debating a rarely used technique that has saved lives during mass casualty events such as the 2017 Las Vegas shooting. It's a protocol that jury-rigs one ventilator for two patients with Y tubing, essentially doubling the number of lives that can be saved. The caveat, however, is that the two patients will share whatever each is breathing in and out, risking an increased viral load to one another.

Could saving lives be worth the risk of harming the very same lives?

Primum non nocere versus "I know not."

In quickly answering this dilemma, however, my friend Alli, a respiratory therapist, forwards guidance released in a statement from the American Association for Respiratory Care. Cosigned by a number of other critical care professional organizations, the statement advises against Y tubing: "It is better to purpose the ventilator to the patient most likely to benefit than fail to prevent, or even cause, the demise of multiple patients."[8]

This is a fancy way of saying "it's better to ration care, namely rationing one ventilator to the single patient who would benefit the most from it," so hospitals may quit arguing about Y tubing and start figuring out the fairest way to decide who lives and who dies. I hear that some will form a committee. Hospitals in other states will implement a lottery system. EMS may be authorized not to transport dying patients, so that the choice is made before they ever get to the ER.

I hear from providers who are running out of medicines: azithromycin, Valium, saline, hydroxychloroquine. The shortage of the last one is a terrible and entirely unnecessary blow to patients with rheumatic conditions who depend on hydroxychloroquine to survive—because there's currently zero strong evidence to prove its clinical efficacy against COVID-19. And how would anyone even know the correct dosage to give at this point of the pandemic? While hoarded toilet paper and stolen masks don't risk blindness or heart arrhythmias, blind dosing with hoarded hydroxychloroquine does. It'll be ironic (and sad, I admit) when people end up catching COVID-19 in my ER because they self-medicated to avoid catching COVID-19.

Primum non nocere versus "I know not."

We also remain low on PPE. Other than personal donations to a few lucky individuals like me, there's no sign of bunny suits or PAPRs like we're seeing standardized in other countries.

If I ever lay hands on this mythical PAPR at this point of the pandemic, I'll probably be dragged to the stake and burned for witchcraft.

Even as we try to do no harm, this world is doing harm to us.

For days now I've also gotten anonymous email solicitations from enterprising people and bots claiming (falsely) to be Makrite or 3M sales reps, offering to sell me N95s in bulk for thousands of dollars. This is true harm and truly abhorrent.

As if we're not dealing with enough bullshit already, now you're trying to profit from our fear and desperation? *Really?*

I get more and more requests for N95s or any other PPE I can get my hands on. Thankfully, I also get messages from more and more friends—Norman, Daniel, Chen—who have shipped PPE for sharing to my apartment. So to each request I can respond: *Tell me when you're free and I'll get you some masks.*

But no matter how much fresh PPE I hand out, it won't solve this, from a medical school friend:

> Just got this from our hospital chair: ICU is at full capacity and we have no more vents. 120 admitted boarding patients are waiting in the ER.

That number takes my breath away. Even though I'm personally bearing witness to—hell, participating in—the same emergency, my mind struggles to wrap itself around 120 people so sick they can't go home packed into a space designed for maybe half that number, and more arriving every hour. Until someone dies to free up a bed, they're stuck.

We're all juggling a million bowling pins at once while unicycling on top of a house of cards in a packed casino of infected patients throwing bowling balls at us.

Welcome to pandemic roulette.

MARCH 26, 2020

"We have a code!"

Habits take over. The resuscitation symphony. . . .

• • •

By 10:30 tonight, the length of stay (LOS) column on the EMR board, which tracks the time a registered ER patient has waited either for discharge or a bed upstairs, looks like this (HH:MM):

06:12	
00:19	
05:16	test pending
02:22	
12:44	positive
01:19	test pending
06:03	
06:24	
05:09	
04:22	test pending
08:29	positive
08:01	
01:35	
04:30	
02:38	
05:58	

06:46	
06:43	
08:54	
15:12	
00:27	
10:33	positive
01:37	
02:51	
05:26	test pending
06:13	
03:10	
02:26	
11:48	
06:02	
07:42	
05:42	
05:18	
04:55	
04:13	test pending
03:38	

03:29	test pending

| 02:11 | |

In case you missed it: Someone with a *confirmed* case of COVID has been in the ER for more than twelve hours and forty-four minutes, because there's nowhere else to go.

On better days, the column to the left of LOS designates a location in the emergency department where the patient can be found. That column is blank today because there is no more space to assign, not even "HALLWAY." *I guess it's good they're not outside? But at this rate . . .*

By eleven, which is six hours into my shift, there have been three deaths here in the ER among admitted patients waiting for beds upstairs. At 1:00 a.m. EMS brings in another who is dead on arrival (DOA). That will make four dead bodies (that we know of) that will keep us company all night in the ER.

Can't stay here, can't go anywhere: I don't want to be here anymore. I don't want to be anywhere anymore.

I decide to take tomorrow off. And maybe the next day.

While I may not want to be anywhere anymore, I still return home where my partner, Mel, has stayed up for support. Far removed from the medical world, she has been grounded, working remotely from the safety of home. Her looks of concern and not knowing what's truly going on agonize me. For the past nineteen days, I have struggled whether to word vomit the raw details of what I've seen behind the walls of our emergency rooms or to protect her from the holy terror. The former feels selfish, the latter feels cowardly. Neither feels wrong.

This dilemma makes me feel like I'm now living the pandemic remake of *The Farewell.* My gut tells me that divulging the whole truth would be cruel. It's as if I finally understand what my own family was doing in protecting me from their skeletons the best way they knew how. What is love if it is not both the desire to reveal whole truths but also protect those from the whole truth? What a paradox.

Is it better to ask if I am respecting them enough to presume they would be able to handle the trauma, or is respect better defined by shouldering the burden so I may keep my loved ones away from the trauma?

There has to be another way. Maybe that's what the time off is for.

MARCH 27, 2020

I get an email informing me that a case, twelve boxes with twenty masks each, of N95s has arrived for me, but it's so big I have to pick it up at the local Duane Reade pharmacy on 79th and 2nd Ave. I open the case right there and start sharing with the pharmacy staff as thanks for letting me make a giant mess on their floor while I figure out a way to get it all home.

I announce on social media, with a photo of the riches:

O O O

If you're a frontline healthcare worker and I know you are one, DM me to pick up a few for yourself and your colleagues.

Within the hour, two emergency residents a couple of years behind me stop by to pick up four boxes each. An intern shows up a few hours later to grab two boxes.

Not bad for a day's worth of work on a day off.

MARCH 28, 2020

Two more deliveries on my second day off, from two different college friends. The first, from Daniel, contains two boxes of 3M bunny suits: two weeks' worth of head-to-toe protection. The second is a full-face P100 that looks like an old-timey underwater dive mask, with a note from Paula:

"Stay safe and see you after this is all over!" I wish them both virtual hugs from afar.

Although this P100 fits a bit small on me, I already have a couple of colleagues in mind who will sing hallelujah on their COVID shifts, especially if it comes time to intubate.

Victoria, a graduating medical student who has shadowed me for work and monsooned with me for fun, then stops by with a bag of Lavazza coffee to exchange for some N95s. It's like a typical drug deal, only with no drugs or money.

I soon get a text from Vyjayanthi, a friend I made right before the pandemic, offering her unoccupied apartment for any frontline healthcare worker wanting to cut down on their pandemic commutes. Two more messages then follow, also meant for the larger healthcare worker community who are following me on social media, so I post on my accounts to help people make badly needed living arrangements:

○○○

My apartment in midtown east is empty right now, I'm at my in-laws' place. If you know of any NYU docs that need a place to stay closer to the hospital or away from their families, I'm happy to lend it. It's bare bones since I was going to sell, but there's an air mattress and a couch, and it's 2 blocks from the hospital.

I have an empty studio that's furnished near Union Square if any doctors need to stay there—close to Beth Israel.

My place is available for trusted people if needed, midtown east of Manhattan.

This is what supporting the frontline looks like. My friends are knocking my socks off. Thank God for high-quality humans.

MARCH 29, 2020

Before today's shift I come across a photo from the 1918 flu pandemic of female nurses assembling makeshift masks for their (presumably male, given the times) doctors. Behind them is a poster that reads: IF I FAIL, HE DIES. I feel encouraged both that we've been through something like this before and that the world has changed for the better since then. Now we're all helping each other, all genders working together. Even if you told me something crazy like World War III were to follow this pandemic, we won't and must not fail each other. We must be part of a world that must always change for better.

In the late morning of my shift, I realize I've seen so many confirmed positive COVID-19 patients—more than 85 percent positive among countless hundreds—in the past twenty days that I no longer need a nasopharyngeal PCR swab to confidently diagnose a new case. I only need to see the following workaround signs in the ER:

1. After a brief walk around the room, a reading of less than 94 percent oxygen saturation and/or you look terrible and are short of breath
2. Low white blood count (leukopenia)
3. X-ray with a bilateral pneumonia pattern

Other doctors are using fancy lab tests I can't easily get my hands on in an ER (as if they were a mythical PAPR). For example, I read about COVID-19 patients whose pattern of blood work would show elevated C-reactive protein and ferritin levels while their procalcitonin levels—a biomarker for infection—remain normal. Whatever methods we use, we're all getting better at identifying the disease without a direct PCR test that still takes a day or two for results (and they're saying that our current PCRs may be only 60 to 70 percent effective at catching positive cases to begin with).

I'm also increasingly able to predict poor outcomes based on the following after a patient has been admitted to the hospital:

1. Elevated inflammatory markers called IL–6, which are predominantly found in fat (adipose) tissue
2. Liver function above five times the upper limit of normal
3. Low platelet counts (thrombocytopenia)
4. Intubation/life support

Also based on my own observations, the cytokine storm that leads to the greatest risk of mortality most often occurs around ten to eleven days after exposure.

Collaborating with other providers on social media, I instruct my staff to modify a few standard protocols based on the outcomes we're seeing among COVID patients:

1. The standard sepsis protocol that involves pushing a large fluid bolus all at once seems to exacerbate respiratory difficulty. Use with discretion.
2. A prone position (lying on the belly instead of the back) seems to provide better oxygenation for patients on supplemental oxygen. Use liberally but monitor carefully.
3. If a patient is at or above 90 to 92 percent oxygen saturation and can do both walking and talking without any effort, they're probably safer quarantining at home where the viral load is bound to be lighter than in a hospital setting (and we can save the bed for someone in acute distress). Use shared decision-making.

In my growing corner of the social media world, other healthcare workers have also been sharing some of the experiences they're having trouble dealing with or letting go.

○○○

An elderly well-appearing patient came into the ER four days ago, sent by his wife for abdominal pain to rule out bowel obstruction. After waiting hours in the ER for a CT scan, obstruction was ruled out and he was discharged. He returned here a day later with fever and cough. He died today.

Do you remember that guy from the group home who was sent in for their chief complaint of "playing with his penis" to rule out a urinary tract infection? Normal urinalysis, discharged as quickly as we could. He's back with covid symptoms, along with their staff member who had first brought him in.

I swear the 20-month-old kid I coded was a false negative for COVID. I just swabbed a corpse. Who knows. They claimed it was "croup" at [another hospital] despite fully negative pathogens panel and flu negative. He was discharged from there with "subtle retractions" and came to our ER dead the next day.

[From a pediatric ER physician:] There have been two YOUNG child deaths but numbers not accurately reported. Many children intubated (two of my patients), many more according to pediatric emergency/ICU listservs. This is far worse than China or Italy.

The LOS column on today's EMR board runs from 17:09 to 51:38. *Fifty-one hours and thirty-eight minutes.* One patient has been here *more than two days.*

I run my face shield and goggles under the faucet once again. The patterned decals on both are chipping off.

9 YEARS AGO

Summer 2011: Whys & Meanings

I notice the paint chips peeling from the walls and ceiling. We are the only two foreigners amongst a sea of local Jordanians. In a balcony cafe awash with the perfumed clouds of narghile haze, our bodies float over the muted chaos of downtown Amman. For a moment, everything seems simple, impossible to deconstruct or analyze. For a moment, everything just *is*, a unit in itself, as if a feather duvet has wrapped us in an eternity for now. Unlike the polished streets of downtown Beirut or the Western commercialism of Istanbul's Beyoğlu, we have finally arrived somewhere that sees no need for haste.

This is Eastern Amman. We go against the countless guidebooks that tell us there really isn't anything to see here, and take in a kind of experience that cannot be written about. What can even a picture do for a thousand words that are unwritable? I can post hundreds of pictures with a camera that supposedly makes real life look better, and it still would not be able to capture a surreal idea of our—well, not just being here, but—just *being*. And it is for this very kind of moment that I have come to travel;

perhaps I've traveled thousands of miles just so I can find this moment. How can I stay here for just a little bit longer?

. . .

Doubt is useful for a while. . . . . But we must move on.

To choose doubt as a philosophy of life is akin to

choosing immobility as a means of transportation.

—Yann Martel, *Life of Pi*

Over the course of six hours, on the bus from Kathmandu to Pokhara, I have finished Yann Martel's *Life of Pi* in one sitting. I am moved by this novel in ways I haven't been since James Joyce's *The Dead*, Gabriel García Márquez's *One Hundred Years of Solitude*, or Joan Didion's *The Year of Magical Thinking* the week of my father's death.

The novel mentions regions I am bound for on this trip (Madurai, Pondicherry) and places I've already been (Munnar, Chennai). But more than that, it chronicles a spiritual journey and nudges at the meaning behind storytelling. I refuse to succumb to the notion that this trip or this blog of mine are attempts to force meaning into life, like some fetishized search for the exotic. But the past few days have offered me greater clarity into why I followed through on that wager that led me to Egypt, why I still applied to medical school despite no longer having the specter of my father looming over my decisions, why my travel blog exists at all, and whatever I have been attempting all along without knowing why or how.

After my dreamlike experience at Petra by night a fortnight ago, my soulful conversations last week in Dubai with Mona (whom I actually had first met months prior at Machu Picchu when she asked me for directions), and reading both *The Alchemist* and *Life of Pi* within the past few days, I have arrived at the idea that the road of life, at least for me, makes more sense as a sum of its parts than as disconnected details. The magic would actually be lost if I thought too hard and too often about what it all means, if I were to "check my pulse" every waking moment. With "one foot in the past and the other foot in the future, you might as well be pissing on the present," they say. My own father died from the terrible irony of checking his blood pressure too often—every elevated reading made him want to check it again, driving up his pressure even higher—and I don't intend to repeat his fatal mistake.

Instead I will have faith and entrust the present and future to the unseen. I will write this all down, whether or not I know "why" or what "it" means, and one day I will look back on the stories posted here and appreciate a unifying form to their madness: I will see an idea made whole from a string of incoherently linked posts. Neville Goddard, a godfather of New Thought, wrote, "Have faith in your imagined act." And so I shall.

It is, of course, at this very moment, when I am writing these words on a rickety local bus under a black Nepalese night sky on a desolate mountain road, that I begin to believe life as a whole can, perhaps, make sense to another wandering soul. It is possible. Maybe I won't feel this way years from now, or tomorrow, or in five minutes, but right now I shall have nothing to do with the uncertainty of the future. It may or may not yet exist. So I live now. And "right now" is whispering to me how meaning can inhabit every single minute we bear our existence. Then when it's the right time, we just have to learn how to reflect hard and deeply when honoring its presence.

So even knowing this, how can my mind train itself to stop wandering to the uncertainty of the future? Instead of forcing upon myself these constant reminders to stay present, can I simply just *know* to stay and enjoy this very eternity moment?

Then again, if it were not for monsooning and travel, I would never have arrived at such an awareness in the first place.

Maybe travel is a practice. A form of meditation.

They call it "monsooning."

And just like an unknown future, this bus rolls on into darkness.

MORBIDITY

~~~~~

March 30–April 15, 2020

n. (mor·bid·i·*tē*) the condition of suffering from a disease; the consequences and complications (other than death) that result from a disease.

MARCH 30, 2020

Since March 8, for the past twenty-three days, every single day this month has felt like one of those open-top tour buses rolling into a different circle of hell. Maybe I'll swap the "z" for an "n" in my middle name to make it *Dante*, for every morning now feels like a recent escape from the inferno of the night before.

On this particular morning, I wake up noticing how my wrists are covered in what look like first-degree chemical burns, irritated by uninterrupted hours in countless pairs of latex and nitrile gloves. Constant friction has dried my skin to the point of burning, another hex from the underworld to match my mask-ravaged nose.

Later, on shift, a nurse I've worked with at a different hospital is in this ER as a patient. She looks in terror at the oxygen monitor's readout. "Is that really my saturation level?"

Five minutes ago, we thought we had her steady at 92 percent. Now, with no supplemental oxygen, she's at 74 percent and dropping. But she still looks well and is talking to me; I want to give her supplemental noninvasive oxygen support and avoid intubation. "How are you feeling?" I ask.

"I don't know if I can't breathe or if I'm having a panic attack, but you and I both know I can't survive at that number. I've seen people with COVID just drop dead after staying at that number for too long."

"We don't have to intubate if we can bring your sats back up. You're speaking fine. Can we prone you?"

"No, I'm sure. Don't waste time proning me. Intubate me now." When you're a healthcare worker as a patient, the conversation changes.

"Are you sure? We can put you in a private room on BiPAP [noninvasive ventilation], and then in a prone position; we've got options. We can do this step-wise and check in. We really don't have to be at that point yet."

"No. Get straight to it, secure my airway and bring my sats up. I'd rather you intubate me; I'll be fine."

My staff moves her to the critical side of the ER to intubate, and I step outside for some fresh air. *Another fallen colleague. How many more?* I picture a day in the future when we look at each other in disbelief and ask, "Did we really go through all that??"

Yeah, we did.

(But I won't get that chance with my just-intubated colleague. She will be dead two days from now.)

. . .

I cover a few late-evening hours in the ER I was in two days ago. The man whose length of stay (LOS) was 51:38 when I left on Sunday has now been waiting for a bed for 70:08. Seventy hours and eight minutes. This ER is now his circle of hell too.

MARCH 31, 2020

The longest LOS guy from last night has now been waiting 82:35 and is still alive. *Three and a half days in an ER.* My hat is off to him. Anyone who lacks his tenacity: Please come back later. Our hospitals are still full.

We hear that the USNS *Comfort* has docked on our shores with a big announcement: They will take only non-COVID patients. At first glance, great! There's now somewhere for people to get emergency treatment for trauma and acute conditions without risking coronavirus exposure. But once you give it a few minutes' thought, the whole idea starts to break down.

The logistics are impossible.

- We hear that our current COVID-19 PCR tests are, at best, 70 percent sensitive, meaning they can miss three in ten positives. In an emergency situation, are they going to make patients wait dockside for hours in the cold (or indoors with other potentially positive COVID patients) for multiple negative PCRs that take at least a few hours, if not days, before they let them on board?
- Some COVID patients present with only abdominal pain or even just diarrhea as a symptom. Will they

refuse patients with any kind of abdominal pain, just to be on the safe side?

- Healthcare workers may be asymptomatic carriers. Will they test every worker every day far enough in advance of their scheduled shift that they can guarantee no one positive for the virus is ever onboard?

Last time there was COVID-19 (or any virus for that matter) on a boat, it did not go well. An intensivist/ICU physician texts me a dire prediction:

This will be a 100% COVID ship in under 3 days.

I can't see how she's wrong. I hear from other HCP both on and off the ship, and nobody seems to think this is a good idea. The *Comfort* is *not* designed or prepared for infection control. Once the virus boards the boat, it'll be a forest fire. Another zombie outbreak.

Zooming out to consider our problems back on terra firma though, it still makes sense why the military would want to do something, anything, to help:

N.Y.C.'s 911 System Is Overwhelmed. 'I'm Terrified,' a Paramedic Says.

THE NEW YORK TIMES, UPDATED MARCH 31, 2020

With coronavirus cases mounting, emergency workers are making life-or-death decisions about who goes to a hospital and who is left behind.[1]

THE REGIONAL EMERGENCY MEDICAL SERVICES COUNCIL OF NEW YORK CITY, INC.

Est. 1974

NYC REMAC

Advisory No.	2020-08
Title:	**TEMPORARY Cardiac Arrest Standards for Disaster Response**
Issue Date:	March 31, 2020
Effective Date:	Immediate
Supersedes:	n/a

Page:	1 of 1

The Regional Emergency Medical Advisory Committee (REMAC) of New York City is responsible to develop, approve and implement prehospital treatment and transport protocols for use within the five boroughs of the City of New York. The Regional Emergency Medical Advisory Committee (REMAC) of New York City operates under the auspices of Article Thirty of the New York State Public Health Law.

The NYC REMAC proudly thanks the EMS Professionals tirelessly working to protect and serve the residents of NYC and recognizes that EMS provides an <u>ESSENTIAL</u> service to this city, state and country.

<u>**Basis:**</u>

In order to ensure the safety of our providers while also providing care to our patients, the following changes have been made in the **Cardiac Arrest** procedure:

- <u>**No**</u> adult non-traumatic or blunt traumatic cardiac arrest is to be transported to a hospital with manual or mechanical compressions in progress without either return of spontaneous circulation (ROSC) or a direct order from a medical control physician <u>unless</u> there is imminent physical danger to the EMS providers on the scene.

- In the event a resuscitation is terminated, and the body is in public view, the body can be left in the custody of NYPD.

- In the event NYPD response is delayed call the following:
  - NYPD DOA Removal: <u>646-610-5580</u>

Current and Updated Protocols can be accessed at the Regional EMS Council website: www.nycremsco.org.

Owners/operators of Ambulance and ALS First Response Services providing prehospital medical treatment within the five boroughs of the City of New York are responsible to provide copies of the NYC REMAC Prehospital Treatment Protocols to their personnel, and to ensure that Service Medical Directors and EMS personnel are informed of all changes/updates to the NYC REMAC Prehospital Treatment Protocols.

Josef Schenker, MD, CPE, FACEP, FAEMS
Chair, Regional Emergency Medical Advisory
Committee of New York City

Marie C. Diglio, BA, EMT-P
Executive Director Operations,
Regional Emergency Medical Services Council
of New York City

We judge ourselves by our intentions

and others by their behavior.

—Stephen Covey

New York's Emergency Medical Services Council released modified protocols earlier today. A friend from EMS dispatch messages me to offer some context for those following my social media:

> It's critical that patients or family members describe all signs and symptoms to the dispatcher so they can triage the call correctly and prioritize an ambulance if the patient isn't stable. They have special response units for unstable or critical patients. But if symptoms don't warrant ER, they're bottom of the barrel for the ambulance line.

Wait, there's an "ambulance line"?

The slippery slope toward medical care rationing just got slipperier. Stay home, people. Stay safe.

I finish one shift and get a call on my way home to help in a different ER, one I've never worked in before. In the cab, I wonder idly if there might be a prize, like for a scavenger hunt, if I can manage to work in every ER in New York City by the time this thing is over. I need a punch card or something. Do I really "gotta catch 'em all"?

I lie in bed at 11:00 p.m., still awake in this last hour of March. Bells of failing mechanical vents give way to poems drifting out, and then I sleep. Or do I *think* I'm asleep? Is this the middle state of consciousness that South Africans call a *dwall*? What kind of nightmares would I be having if I weren't already living in one?

look alive.
You see an oak tree blossoming in my hand
with effortless wonder
as I
look toward new dawns
and magenta skies.
But you don't know how you ended up here
on this stretcher,
grasping the questions
"why me"
"why now"
"why this"
questions that haunt your
soul
and dying breaths.
Among the alarms
you stumble for answers
when you close your eyes
for the last time
when your heartbeats no longer feel your heart, beat
when you no longer hear your lungs breathe
when you forever sleep
when you now hold my dreams awake

and silently screaming to be freed,
I lie awake to your screams.

APRIL 1, 2020

Screw March. It's a new month. I'm punching COVID-19 in the face today.

I feel fired up until I arrive for my midmorning shift, at which time COVID-19 jumps out crying "April Fool's!" and punches *me* in the face again. My day begins with running out of surgical caps and hairnets, so it's back to the CDC's fashion column. I wrap my head in my souvenir scarf, don my bunny suit, strap on my mask, and tape gloves to my suit. *Six minutes. A record. I'm getting better at this.*

I hand off my extra scuba-like P100 mask to my colleague Diana. We're headed out to the COVID-19 tent and reviewing our treatment plan: Release as quickly as possible. If a patient is walking, talking, speaking full sentences, and boasts normal vital signs, they better start planning their ride home. *Anywhere is safer than here. You need to wait around for a test like you need a bug living in your ear . . . as if that would be another symptom of COVID.*

After three hours, we've discharged more patients than we've admitted and we're feeling good about ourselves. *COVID's under new management.*

I post an infographic on social media that shows how a sneeze or cough causes droplets to travel far more than six feet in the air and remind people to keep their distance. In response I hear from Hudson, a colleague I trained with two years ago, who has done a quick and dirty revision. His caption reads, "This is how my wet farts travel." I push it to my followers. If imagining a wet fart inspires people to maintain physical distance, that works for me. Farts are funny. You laugh, you remember better.

The sun is shining when I step outside for a break, and I do a little dance to celebrate. Someone catches me, as I'll see later on social media, but right now I'm just in the moment.

For only a moment, though, because a few minutes later EMS rolls in with a thirty-year-old woman who can't lift her left hand or see properly out of both eyes. We call a stroke code. *A thirty-year-old*—thirty-year-old!—*having a stroke. As if that would be another symptom of COVID?*

Around 4:00 p.m. I have a chance to see what's left for lunch among the platters of donated restaurant food: a chicken leg, half a chicken breast, a dollop of salad. I don't want to eat near patients or even in the breakroom with my mask off, so I balance my plate on a safety bollard outside. Lunch table, *et voilà!* It takes me another five minutes to un-tape and de-suit myself enough to eat. *Solid deterrent against stress eating.*

I scan local headlines as I chow down. Governor Cuomo has signed Executive Order 202.10, which temporarily grants frontline healthcare providers blanket legal immunity (except in cases of deliberate and gross negligence), lifts the attending level MD or DO-supervision requirement for PAs and nurse practitioners, and dials back the thorough (and some would argue onerous) charting requirements that are New York's standard of care. This is a bold but sadly necessary move. Responding well to COVID-19 patients requires health workers to bring our best to the worst situation with an unknown number of unknowns. For most of us, our best will be better if we don't have to constantly fear fucking up. There's nothing like the threat of a malpractice suit waiting for us after (or even during) a pandemic to keep bone-tired, underresourced, doing-our-damnedest healthcare providers home from work (they'll probably still be waiting for us anyway).

It's the pandemic version of the Good Samaritan Law.

A second overflow tent is going up next to this one. *It's that bad already?* I hear that the first is for testing patients who don't need to be in the ER, while the second will be for admitted patients for whom there are no beds in the hospital.

"Feels like two weeks too late," I remark.

"Better late than never."

"Agreed. Can I work in the tents from now on? Seems safer than in the ER," I say, gesturing to the built-in negative pressure system. The irony is lost on none of us: Impromptu disaster relief tents outside in the elements under incoming April showers now feel safer than our brick-and-mortar emergency departments.

So much irony these days; life itself is ironic. And at this rate, I have no choice but to respect its machinations.

On my cab ride home just before midnight, I peel off my PPE one piece at a time. I feel like the Terminator and all his parts, but instead of eye surgery, I'm pulling at the pulp that used to be my nose. A text from Diana comes in: "Thanks for making me laugh today!! Really kept my morale up. You da best."

A friend I haven't seen since high school waits outside my door.

"Oh my gosh, how long has it been?!"

"Good to see you alive, man." *How's that for a greeting these days?* "Here's some stuff left over from our work back during 9/11. Figured you could use them more than me right now."

It's a bag full of P100 masks and filters. His trash is my treasure. I remember how he used to torment me back in middle school, and now he's saving my life. Mine and so many others. "Thank you, man," I say, sincerely.

"No worries. You look tired. Go to bed."

And just like that he's gone. I haven't seen him since.

APRIL 2, 2020

I celebrate a morning off by making breakfast instead of ransacking old boxes of donated pizza. I'm so pumped that I try for the first time ever to flip an egg in the pan. It lands on the floor. Nala, my kitten, watches in bemusement. "I can't believe it either," I tell her with my thumb proudly pointed to my chest. "They put *me* in charge of emergency rooms during a pandemic." Nala blinks. She's my Wilson from *Castaway*. At least she can meow back and won't float away.

As if the universe was taking pity on my pizza and kitchen-floor-marinated egg diet, a few hours later I receive a shipment of gourmet frozen noodle soups from my friend Jenny, who has been working to not only get PPE for healthcare workers but also making sure I get fed when cooking eggs may seem daunting.

Happily securing my immediate dietary future, I scroll through messages sent from around the world and push them to social media:

○ ○ ○

Australia here, we haven't even started yet and we've already run out. Hospitals telling physicians they can't wear their own masks, my friend is on covid shift and brought her own PAPR. There will be lots of negligence death lawsuits but the right to sue will die with the person.

[in response] It's true unfortunately. We don't have near enough PPEs to get our hospitals through this in Australia. We're nowhere near USA's stats but it won't be long the way we're going. I'm clerical staff, mainly in ED, renal and maternity, and they don't seem to think it's enough of a risk for non-clinical staff to "waste" a mask or gloves, etc. I get that we're not clinical staff, but I'd like to think our lives and our families matter! We all play our part and we work damn hard, too.

A picture sent from Kyrgyzstan shows a fast-food worker behind a soda machine wearing a head-to-toe bunny suit and N95. They've got better PPE in their McDonald's than we've got in our hospital.

I get two back-to-back calls around 7:00 p.m. asking if I can cover shifts at two different hospitals for doctors down with COVID, one of whom had appeared to be in recovery until a serious rebound. Another request comes in around 9:00 p.m. Which one do I accept, if any at all?

I can't help but remember that scene in *Black Hawk Down* when the gunner gets shot and the sergeant immediately yells for somebody to take his place at the turret—and the remaining company members glance around at each other not sure if the sergeant really meant to "take his place" at the turret or getting shot, and understandably hesitate to climb up there into the line of fire.

We are the walking dead.

As I decide that I want to think about something else, another package filled with Trader Joe's instant coffee arrives thanks to Roxanne, a friend who crashed at my place a few years ago during those pre-COVID halcyon days of carefree abandon. Perfect timing. Thanks, Roxanne.

APRIL 3, 2020

I settle for the wake-up consolation prize (no sore throat or fever, hooray!) since the grand prize (a full night of restful sleep) isn't in the cards. My taxi driver blasts "New York City" by the Chainsmokers as the Brooklyn Bridge emerges on our left down FDR Drive. It's just about perfect: "New York City / please go easy / on me."[2] Amen.

I'm spritzing down my computer at an ER I've run before, taking instructions from the overnight doc to look after his patients that are still waiting for results. He mutters his way down the list of patients still waiting for test results before a medical disposition can be decided. I look at one of them as he's talking and notice something . . . off.

"Is he . . . alive?"

He glances over and gets up, "Lemme check." He returns a few seconds later and says, "Yeah, I forgot we had to call it. Could you let his family know? It's been a long night."

I thought I was way beyond shockable, but this is next level. This dude just asked me to inform the family of a patient who died during *his* shift. "A long night?" There is a pause. Then when it doesn't seem he'll follow up with a response, I continue, "I don't think it's appropriate that you would ask me to explain what happened to the family of a patient I didn't even see or take care of."

A nurse taps me on the shoulder and pulls me by the elbow to another patient as the overnight doctor slinks away. "I don't know what's wrong with him," the nurse says, "but he was in *way* over his head. We pronounced that patient at least twenty minutes ago. We don't trust any of the new guys they're sending in."

I'd be informed by my colleagues a couple days later that the hospital and the overnight doctor would contentiously part ways. Maybe better for both parties involved?

I spend the next hour trying to contact the deceased's family, not my favorite way to begin a shift. In between patients and listening to voice mail greetings, a different nurse comes over. "I didn't want to interrupt you on the phone, Calvin, but there's a giant hole in the back of your bunny suit."

"Oh, God. How embarrassing. Do you mind taping it up for me?"

My back is crisscrossed with tape, and I double-wrap my ankle covers and gloves while we're at it. My suit is secure. My emotions are not. I take a minute to breathe, hand a spare P100 to my PA, Nicolette, and tell myself to get going. We got this. Seventy-seven patients on the board in an ER designed for forty. *Let's light this candle.*

Around 8:30 a.m., an older gentleman in a white coat introduces himself. "Dr. Sun, I'm Dr. Smith, an old surgeon way past his prime who's been doing hernia repairs for twenty years. All our elective surgeries have been canceled, as I'm sure you know, but I can't just sit around on my hands and do nothing while you ER guys get all the attention."

I look at him in surprise. "You *volunteered?* Is it worth the risk?"

He shrugs good-naturedly. "I guess we'll find out. Sure beats sitting around doing nothing. Look, I know I'm way older than you, but this is your domain and you're my boss. Tell me what to do, and I'll do it." What a mensch.

This crisis is bringing out the very best and the very worst of us. Not long after Dr. Smith joins our shift, an anesthesiologist also volunteering with us downstairs informs me that another patient has been pronounced dead in the ER. He'd been waiting more than sixty hours for a bed upstairs. I confirm his time of death and get on the phone again. As it rings, I scan the EMR board for a fresh lay of the land. One patient's chief complaint is in the system as "Symptoms." Helpful.

"We have a code! Someone's coding outside in the waiting room!" I slam down the receiver and run toward the waiting room, until I see a nurse half the size of the patient hauling him into the main ER. We lower the bedrails and get him onto the closest open stretcher. No pulse.

"Start CPR!"

As I confirm everyone's roles and place pads on the patient's chest, the nurse fills me in. "I saw his family bring him into the waiting room and get him into a chair; he just slumped over. Something didn't look right. They looked clueless and didn't know what to do; they don't know how long he's been down. His heart could've stopped on the cab ride over here for all I know."

We push meds and pause for a pulse check, the monitor showing a quivering falsetto string. "V. fib., resume compressions while the AED charges." When the defibrillator hits 360J and a light flickers on to show it's ready, I call out, "Everyone clear?"

All hands off, everyone confirms, "Clear!"

"Shocking."

Our patient flinches with 360 joules of electricity.

"Resume compressions!"

Wash, rinse, repeat. CPR, meds, pause for pulse check. We shock him again and the monitor picks up a rhythm. We've got his heart, but the results of his blood gas test come back:

pH level (normal 7.4): < 6.80. *Incompatible with life.*

Potassium level (normal 3.5 to 5.0): 6.9. *Nearly incompatible with life.*

Lactate level (normal <1.7): >19.0. *Incompatible with life.*

We intubate to protect his airway and have the mechanical ventilator breathe for him. The following chest X-ray reads, "Bilateral ground glass opacities consistent with viral pneumonia and probable coronavirus/COVID-19 pattern. Status post intubation; endotracheal tube in appropriate position."

I head to the waiting room to give his family the sad news. They have a hard time getting past my bunny suit to hear what I'm saying, and ask if they can come in to say goodbye. I shake my head, "As much as I wish you could be with your loved one when he passes, exposing yourself to higher doses of COVID-19 is not a safe choice. I don't want you to be back here in two weeks like him." This takes a few moments to register, but eventually they nod. They'll head home and FaceTime his last moments. They've been hearing about that option on the news.

Hanane, the next PA to start her shift, arrives to lighten our patient load. I then take a breather and check my messages. Someone has forwarded an article from a few days ago that brings a rush of hot tears to my eyes:

Woman, 90, dies from coronavirus in Belgium after refusing a ventilator and telling doctors, "I had a good life, keep this for the younger."[3]

A group text with medical school colleagues careens from sadness to fear to an anxious reminder that, even though we're all just over thirty, we should have our wills completed ASAP. Of course it's true, but *Damn, is our premature loss of innocence another circle of hell?*

Around 2:00 p.m. EMS drops off an awake, alert, irritable ninety-year-old man well known to the neighborhood for frequent public intoxication. On one hand I'm glad someone out there is still living his best life. But on the other, is exposing a nonagenarian to a COVID-riven ER really the best thing for him? We put him in a chair outside with a few warmed blankets to breathe fresh air and sober up.

EMS wasting a trip on this guy is extra ironic given the headlines: "NYC emergency medical services to stop taking unresponsive cardiac patients to hospitals."[4] So if your family member's heart stops and you call 911, new policy dictates they won't be brought in . . . but a ninety-year-old drunk gets a lift whether he wants it or not.

They bring him back inside around 5:30 p.m. because "a bystander called 911," not realizing we actually *wanted* him outside where he might not die. I feel sympathy for the EMS personnel but the concerned upstanding citizen who called 911 needs a physically distanced kick in the ass; I know what they mean when they say the road to hell is paved with good intentions.

I get a call from my friend and chief neurologist who assumed care of the thirty-year-old woman for whom we had called a stroke code a couple of days ago. She is now permanently paralyzed on one side from an embolism in her carotid artery. Aside from being COVID-positive, she had no other conditions that commonly lead to stroke, and my colleague sends along some early, provisional research linking COVID-19 both to encephalopathy (damage to the brain) and thrombophilia (a tendency to develop blood clots). *So that could have been COVID too. This shit is crazy.* I don't know what to believe anymore. How does this virus even work?

By the time my shift is over, we've whittled seventy-seven morning patients down to twenty, more often now by discharging people safely home rather than pronouncing them dead. Is that progress? Hailing a cab, I rip the tape off on my face and it takes skin with it.

About the time I get home, my grandfather calls. He has a fever and a cough. He is also eighty-five years old.

No no no no no no no no no no.

He asks if he should go to the hospital. I point out that he's speaking full and clear sentences without hesitation or shortness of breath and seems to have his normal level of energy. No, he should definitely *not* go to the hospital where he will be exposed to higher doses of virus. I'll come over with a pulse oximeter and monitor him from home. He says no, and sounds confused by my insistence for him not to go to an emergency room.

I soon hear from my mother that he had called 911 anyway for an ambulance to Elmhurst Hospital. Not long later a text comes through from a college buddy and second-year resident I've worked with named Debashree, who happens to be on rotation at Elmhurst. They've admitted my grandfather because of his age and because he told every healthcare staff member in the ER that I'm his grandson. Not helpful.

My stomach ties in knots. I feel so helpless. He shouldn't be there! But friends console me how he had decided for himself, and that medical ethics would compel me from directly and presumptively intervening in his care.

Mom said my grandfather, a doctor himself, was convinced that hospitals "can fix everything." I hope he's right. But I know I'm not wrong.

APRIL 4, 2020

As if we were all scratching the days on the wall of a jail cell, I count the days and it's now day 28 with the same shit, different ER. (Literally: My first patient is that same happily drunk ninety-year-old who can't get a moment's peace from emergency services.) Every morning now feels like the scene from *Aliens* where Ellen Ripley gears up in the elevator.

But now my grandfather is a COVID-19 patient at Elmhurst Hospital, the pandemic epicenter of Queens of the country's pandemic epicenter of New York City. That's new. That's personal.

Every phone in the city, including mine, buzzes at 2:30 p.m.:

EMERGENCY ALERT
Attention all healthcare workers: New York City is seeking licensed healthcare workers to support healthcare facilities in need. Visit NYC.gov/help now to volunteer.

Pretty sure I'm already doing that, but okay?

One of today's tasks is to call patients who came to the ER during the past week for COVID-19 testing and were sent home as quickly as possible. Somebody has to contact them with test results, and today that somebody is me. When I'm unable to reach a patient, I make a note on their chart for follow-up. There's also a string of patient charts with this note copied and pasted over and over:

COVID-19/BioFire Results: POSITIVE
Patient is deceased.

COVID-19/BioFire Results: POSITIVE
Patient is deceased.

COVID-19/BioFire Results: POSITIVE
Patient is deceased.

We get word a little later during these callbacks that a patient who had tested positive for COVID-19 was transferred to the USNS *Comfort* by mistake.

I ask my PA, Katie, if she'll spritz down my bunny suit with alcohol before I take it off. "I'd be honored," she says, taking my bottle in one hand and hers in the other to spray me double-fisted like a John Woo action hero. "Dude, can you not smell this alcohol?" She shoots my face as a joke.

I can't, actually. This P100 is next level.

APRIL 5, 2020

Finally.

New York is merging all its hospitals to battle the coronavirus.

"We're in an almost apocalyptic crisis, which requires cutting through bullshit."[5]

Through four weeks of ER-hopping, working almost as many different systems as hospitals, I think it's crystal clear that we're all supposed to be on the same team, going through the same shit, working with—not competing against—each other. So glad someone up there also finally gets it! Get rid of the medical red tape and bloated bureaucracy tying our hospital systems in knots, and we might actually kick this pandemic in the ass. Why couldn't they have done this earlier?

At the same time, I can also see clearly how just one or two bad apples, whether political or medical, could screw it up for all of us and bring the whole effort down. We're all depending on each other, out of nothing but necessity. It's beautiful, and also terrifying.

APRIL 6, 2020:
THE "BACK-AND-FORTH"

Midmorning I walk into today's ER and see nothing but a row of empty stretchers. *What the fuck?*

"Yeah, man," says the overnight doctor. He can read my incredulity even behind my P100. "It's been like this all morning. Don't jinx it."

The never-ending movie reel in my mind cues up "The guns—they've stopped!" from *Star Wars: A New Hope*, and I remind myself that the Death Star's guns cease only because Darth Vader and the variants of his TIE Fighter wingmen are screaming up from behind.

But then I think some more and do a bit of envelope math, realizing that lockdown went into effect fifteen days ago on March 22. If the virus takes between two and five days on average to incubate and make a person symptomatic, with eleven to fourteen days for the outliers and hospital systems finally working together, then this is exactly what we would hope to see as a result of our collective efforts both during and two weeks after a lockdown: a decompressed ER. A flattened curve. *Could we really have done it? Is this our winter solstice?*

My sense of relief wants to feel unbridled joy, untainted by the knowledge that healthcare workers lose both by being right and by being wrong about the predictions associated with a pandemic. If we're wrong, and our dire warnings turn out to be a case of overblown hysteria that has left us with spare ventilators and massive economic fallout, we will be vilified and mistrusted in the future. Alas, there is no glory in prevention.

If, on the other hand, we're right . . . Oh boy, being wrong now feels better than being right. Because "right" is burning bodies in the street while the few remaining doctors and nurses cry out like exhausted prophets, "We warned you but you didn't listen!" And they'd ignore us anyway.

To paraphrase *The Dark Knight*, we either die as heroes ignored, or live long enough to become villains condemned.

Less than an hour later, my worry (hope?) that our hue and cry were all for nothing evaporates. The symptom column of the EMR starts to look familiar:

Shortness of breath
Respiratory distress
Respiratory distress
Respiratory arrest
Respiratory distress

So the curve has not flattened, it just took a breather for a few hours? I feel at once grieved. But mostly aggrieved. The fear of literally stacking corpses is still worse than figuratively being thrown under the bus.

As if to confirm the maxim, someone in Ecuador sends a photo of a dead body wrapped in blankets, stretched out on a bus stop bench. A sign is pinned to the blanket: HEMOS LLAMADO AL 911 Y NO HAY AYUDA. *We called 911 and there is no help.* According to my source, "The government is picking up 150 bodies every day from streets and houses in addition to those who die in hospital."

Here at home we may have a higher body count—*NYT* says it was 425 yesterday—but we've also got field hospital tents, volunteer clinicians, hospitals outside the city accepting patient transfers, upstairs PAs and NPs coming down to treat ER patients, and NYC rising to the occasion. Maybe we really *can* turn the corner on this thing?

By evening, the corner is looking far off again. The back-and-forth. We're swamped again here, and I get several messages from different hospitals reporting a shortage of patient stretchers. Why? Because they're all occupied by the deceased still strapped to them, waiting their turn to go into refrigerator trucks. Guess some uptown colleagues on call tonight will be sleeping on the floor. If they have a chance to sleep at all.

As my shift ends, someone forwards me a tweet from Gov. Cuomo, announcing that COVID patients will now be treated on the good ship USNS *Comfort*: "This means 1,000 additional beds staffed by federal personnel. This will provide much-needed relief to our over stressed hospital systems."[6] Even the USNS *Comfort* is going through its own slipstream of back-and-forth indecisiveness.

So my ICU friend was wrong: It actually took seven days, not three, to become a 100 percent COVID ship. What a pessimist.

APRIL 7, 2020

My doorbell rings just before 10:00 a.m., and a young woman I've never met before drops off a bag of reusable (as in, designed to be used repeatedly unlike the original expectation for an N95 mask) hard face shields, on behalf of an EMT colleague named Everett. Woohoo! One month of fighting this fire and now I can finally toss the flimsy disposable piece of plastic I've been attempting to soap down and reuse for the past three weeks. It's the piece of equipment I've had the longest and thus I feel a little sentimental about letting it go—but then I notice the blue foam headband has turned a sickly shade of green and decide, yes, it's time. Or maybe I should keep it for a museum?

My Iron Man suit of reusable-on-purpose PPE is now fully assembled. A month or so late, but who's counting?

I'm called in on my day off but not to treat patients. I'll be putting together a new weapon for our fight against COVID-19: a closed-circuit CPAP machine with viral filters. Dreamed up by the MacGyvers at the emergency medicine podcast and blog *EMCrit*, it's a breathing apparatus jury-rigged to deliver high-pressure supplemental oxygen without having to intubate.[7] With these beauties, the hope is that we can support patients longer before we have to sedate and paralyze them for mechanical ventilation, keeping more patients awake and reserving ventilators for those who truly won't live without them. The modifications we're making today—filters plus vented plastic sheeting to surround patients—will keep the virus-laden exhalations of infected people contained in a closed system, rather than allowing them to spew into the air for others to inhale.

Win-win-win! Yes, I'd like my cake and to eat it, too, please.

At some point we hear that a *Comfort* crew member has tested positive. This news leads us to chew over the pandemic outlook from here.

That things are "better" this week is relative: Put sugar on feces, it's still feces. That goes at least double for the concept of "plateauing," which the media seems to be so hot on today. The math of a plateau is still akin to taking a bowel movement when you think about it: simple fluid dynamics. If 100 new patients came in yesterday, a plateau means another 100 will come in today. Certainly that's better than 120 today and 140 tomorrow—which was the past three weeks—but it's still far more than the 30 or 40 per day that this ER was designed to handle. And because it takes an average of seven to twelve days—sometimes up to twenty—for an admitted COVID-19 patient to recover, hospitals will keep getting fuller even at 100 today, 100 tomorrow. So plateau or no plateau, purgatory is far from paradise.

What we really need is a dip, a clear and measurable drop in new cases, that lasts long enough for us to discharge a bunch of recovered patients before we must cope with the second wave that's all but inevitable when lockdown is lifted (penciled in for the end of the month). Without a dip, people will not only die in waiting rooms in May; they'll die on the streets with signs taped to their bodies.

I'm also catastrophizing about our own mental health if this doesn't let up, imagining the short- and long-term toll on frontline healthcare workers. How can we feel safe going to work when our safety is so clearly not a priority? Will we still be expected to roll with these conditions if the next pandemic is as contagious as COVID-19 but as lethal as Ebola? How will we recover from the PTSD that results from this traumatic, stress-filled, disordered shit show while still paying off $200,000 to $500,000 in school loans and hoping not to become disabled or, you know, dead? And where are our PAPRs?

CNN's Anderson Cooper interviews me later today and asks how I function while feeling fear in the face of these challenges—because man, I *feel* it: My old friend is back with a vengeance. Anderson probably even senses it over the Cisco Webex signal.

I take a breath and tell him what I keep telling myself: It wouldn't be considered a challenge in the first place if there was no fear preceding it. Therefore concepts such as "courage" could not exist in the absence of fear. So whenever fear rears its head, courage can be a choice. My next choice.

And when I'm afraid but still have courage to go in, maybe that's love.

APRIL 8, 2020

This morning I'm setting up iPads on stands to expand an ER's telemedicine capabilities, so that older and higher-risk healthcare providers can get in on the action from the relative safety of their private offices. We need all hands-on deck, even if the hands are virtual and poorly lit.

As I work, I mull over one possible implication of EMS's hands-off policy regarding cardiac arrests: We may be undercounting deaths in New York City. If no one is bringing us coding patients to be resuscitated or pronounced dead, are those folks included in the daily toll?

The answer, it turns out, is no.

Staggering Surge of NYers Dying in Their Homes Suggest City Is Undercounting Coronavirus Fatalities

Another 200 city residents are now dying at home each day, compared to 20 to 25 such deaths before the pandemic, said Aja Worthy-Davis, a spokeswoman for the medical examiner's office. And an untold number of them are unconfirmed [for coronavirus].[8]

At-home deaths have multiplied tenfold during a worldwide pandemic, but we're just not sure what could be causing it? My, that *is* a mystery.

A few messages on my socials attest and confirm the undercounting both in the city and beyond New York:

○ ○ ○

A good friend of mine lost her partner three days ago waiting for an ambulance—presumably COVID but up until a rapid decline the morning of their death, symptoms weren't bad enough to warrant testing or going to the ER per doctor's advice. As far as my friend knows, their cause of death hasn't been formally determined so isn't counted in the COVID stats.

[From a private EMT driver:] EMS call volume still extremely overwhelming. Maybe slightly better but a LOT don't get transported. Constant cardiac arrests coming over the radio, definitely a lot not being "counted."

[FDNY on Instagram:] During my last tour, every single call was cardiac arrest. Numbers seem to have quadrupled from normal operations.

My husband is a police officer in Michigan and we just talked about this. He said they have had home deaths the coroner

---

ruled as "natural," but the victim had COVID symptoms. He had one case just yesterday.

I remember being gobsmacked by a headline from China way back in February, and less than two months later it's also happening here:

Coronavirus: Why many deaths will never appear in official figures

Wuhan's overburdened health workers are unable to confirm many of those who died were suffering from Covid-19, so they will not show up in official figures.

The families of those who die at home are also denied the comfort of being able to make proper funeral arrangements.[9]

APRIL 9, 2020

I rest a little easier today knowing that I haven't been the only healthcare worker who always felt reluctant about tossing around mechanical ventilation like aspirin or TUMS—public health officials are finally starting to get skeptical too. "Officials in New York City say up to 80 percent of COVID-19 patients placed on machines died. . . . Mechanical ventilation, which forces oxygen into a patient's lungs after they are sedated [and don't forget paralyzed!], can damage lung sacs over time."[10]

Causation or correlation? That's still up for the jury to ultimately decide but four out of five, damn! Any doctor who
isn't alarmed by that statistic is asleep at the wheel. It's been
nearly a month since my first near-intubation of a patient that
had ended up signing out against medical advice, and I now
feel a little more vindicated. I'm going to continue my policy
of delaying intubation until there are literally no other options to keep a patient alive. Validation has been hard to
come by these days.

Today we've got twenty-seven patients on our board. At the
same time last week, we had seventy. Three cheers for quarantining! The guns, maybe they really have stopped.

> Shortness of Breath (Pt's . . .)

> Shortness of Breath (states . . .)

> Shortness of Breath (Pt states . . .)

> Shortness of Breath (Pt states . . .)

And yet triage is still copying and pasting these chief complaints on our board.

By early evening the symptom column on the board in-
cludes not only two dozen respiratory complaints like we've
seen for weeks on end, but also a toothache as well. I silently
cheer to myself; I acknowledge it's odd to feel optimistic
about a toothache, let alone bittersweet to see a non-COVID
symptom from the before-times.

A few minutes before the end of my shift, I overhear another patient without COVID symptoms explain to the recep-
tionist that he's here for a prescription refill and a note for

work. "I don't believe this virus is real," he preemptively announces. He then takes a second to enjoy the hit of dopamine from the attention that his conspiracy statement evoked, before capitalizing on his new high, "and even if it was, I don't care if I catch it and expose my dad to the virus! He told me he doesn't care either!"

His grin is wide, his eyes even wider; he now seems to relish in the passively captive audience to his mania. *So this is how an addiction starts.* "And I don't think we'd ever care if he died, because then I'll be rich afterwards!"

Nobody asked you. *Cool story, bro.*

APRIL 10, 2020

Even as lockdown appears to be making a dent in ER visits, the death toll continues to climb. Given SARS-CoV-2's longer course of disease, death and recovery rates will inevitably be lagging indicators, always a couple of weeks behind case counts.

We may have a handful of reasons to be hopeful here in Manhattan, but I keep hearing from providers in the outer boroughs and they're not all seeing the same promising trends—which makes sense. There is a ton of disparity between neighborhoods, as my own experience in various ERs corroborates. Not all communities are impacted equally by the virus or offered equal access to care. This stressed-out text from an intern in Queens typifies some of what's unfolding elsewhere:

Omg my last overnight was horrible!!! I had 13 myself (it was just me and 2 attendings). the board was nonstop 45-50 patients all night, it was so bad I didn't step out of there till 5:43AM to get a breath of air. I legit was tachypneic after the last code. . . . we kept discovering patients fully awake while intubated or hypoxic one step away from crashing cuz our oxygen ran out and no one noticed. Seriously hope it's getting better cuz that was the worst night since I've been working.

On the other hand, I receive a message from Jacobi Medical Center in the Bronx, where I completed my emergency medicine residency:

Today marks the first COVID-19 patient we successfully extubated and discharged home.

Just maybe, as this thing drags on, we're now learning how to take care of people better.

APRIL 13, 2020

"April showers bring May flowers."

What's left of non-COVID related news in these times has predicted incoming rainstorms, and I find myself hoping the makeshift hospital tents can hold through the coming gales. As squalls descend and lockdown dreams intensify, my tempest of feelings sorts itself into soliloquies, as usual. Lockdowns can do that to a fragile amygdala, let alone the dreams from which they derive.

Naval warfare when millions of thunder droplets make kamikaze runs against the defenses of panes of glass; the windows of your cab appear as if they're making a desperate escape attempt as the night sky roars above you with sense-shattering light and sound.

Your vehicle takes brief refuge underneath a tunnel, surviving the myriad hydro-missiles that hurl themselves upon anything reckless enough to be caught under the storm.

Then as lightning flashes across the tapestry of battleship gray, you find yourself in a reverie of loneliness, wandering an empty city, witnessing this spectacular image of nature at war with mankind.

Indifference and entitlement are forces of human nature at least as destructive as the force of nature begetting these April showers. I write so I don't forget. So I don't become an indifferent seed of new and more brutal storms.

I realized this morning that I've hit a numb stride. I've made a ramshackle routine out of an extraordinary disorder. It's been a week since waking every morning in a cold sweat, wondering if it would be the day I started coughing. Now I no longer give my paranoia much thought as I roll out of bed, suit up as Frankenstein the Easter Bunny, jump into a rideshare where the driver doesn't bat an eye at my spacesuit, clear healthy patients out of ERs as quickly as possible like dust bunnies at spring cleaning, eat a quick meal outside next to refrigerator trucks filled with the dead, and do what I can to keep people from dying. Including myself.

And even by breaking a routine with a new one, I still hate routines; they make life fly by so fast that you forget to stop and smell the roses. So today I step outside in the middle of my shift for a moment to myself and to stop and smell the air of rosy downtown Manhattan. Through the barrel of his camera lens, I lock eyes with a passerby. *Click.* I breathe, and we both know, for now, that we're still alive.

APRIL 14, 2020

Hey Dr. Sun! You might not remember us but you've worked with us before—my colleague remembers you from when he was a med student and I was your intern last September. Small world!

Oh hey! It feels like everyone who's been taking care of him at Elmhurst has worked with me, it sure is a small world.

Yeah! Elmhurst is that kind of place. Anyways, your grandfather is doing much better, but now that he's stronger he's starting to frustrate the staff by pulling off his oxygen mask and pulling out his IV because they're uncomfortable.

Isn't that a good sign that he might be ready to go home?

> His behavior is causing his oxygen levels to drop and he doesn't seem to care.

>> *Oh.*

> So is it okay if we sedate him for his safety?

>> *This must be awkward, asking to sedate your attending's grandpa on Instagram DMs. Can we talk on the phone?*

A few hours later a PA colleague of mine Claire tags me on social media about an undisclosed patient I had just transferred this morning to another hospital due to lack of beds: "#DirectAdmit I gotchu," she writes. *Another small world moment.*

Clearly, I'm not the only one who's hitting a stride. All over the city, colleagues in other ERs and health systems are taking more stable patients into their wards so sick people don't have to wait fifty-two hours in mine. This is what teamwork looks like. We're making it through this shit show together.

APRIL 15, 2020

First day off in almost a week. Victoria drops by my apartment again with more PPE and shoe covers. I yell out my congratulations on her upcoming medical school graduation, the ceremonies for which have unfortunately been curtailed due to the pandemic, do a dance at the curb as she pulls up, and she posts it on her social media, tagging me:

○ ○ ○

DELIVERING PPE TO THIS GUY. I THINK HE'S LOST IT.

Maybe I "lost it" a long time ago, but people like her make me feel found again.

6 YEARS AGO

Spring 2014: Transitions

ADDRESS TO GRADUATES ON THE OCCASION OF SUNY
DOWNSTATE COLLEGE OF MEDICINE COMMENCEMENT,
CARNEGIE HALL, MAY 28, 2014, 9:00 A.M.

When I was applying to medical school, my pre-med advisor told us: "Look to your left. Now look to your right. Chances are, neither of them is going to be a doctor." I felt deeply uncertain whether I'd be one of the few who made it, and so, looking for reassurance, I turned to a fellow pre-med friend and told her how hard I'd been studying for the GRE. She furrowed her brow and shook her head. "Med students take the MCAT. You're prepping for the wrong test."

I was definitely not reassured, but I *was* grateful. That same friend later helped me get a spot in an emergency medicine volunteer program at Bellevue Hospital Center, an experience that led me to choose emergency medicine as my specialty.

She is not here today. My generous friend Sonia, who made sure I studied for the correct exam for medical school, died from an aggressive form of breast cancer at the age of twenty-four. She was vibrant and beautiful, and she's the reason I'm standing here today.

Sonia's life and legacy remind me that, from the very beginning, I could not have done this on my own. Even since we lost her, she has been with me every step of the way—especially when I have felt most alone. Everyone graduating today knows what that feels like in some way. When our vocation as healers feels daunting, overwhelming, at times even impossible, we remind ourselves of the countless people who have believed in us more than we ourselves have believed.

We share today's achievement with loved ones like Sonia.

Medicine is a noble practice, but it is not perfect. It can be good, but it is not always fair. Let us keep its shortcomings in mind as we labor to improve our shared practice. Hippocrates himself would accept nothing less than a continuous desire to expand, deepen, and pass on our knowledge and craft.

As we continue to grow and learn as doctors, we will confront situations that force us to assess and diagnose the world in terms that aren't simply black or white, right or wrong. We must therefore strive to find beauty and meaning in gray areas, and revel in the nuances and complexities that make medicine not just a science but also an art.

It is rarely simple, but simple is not what we signed up for.

In medical school they taught us to think like doctors, but I hope we never forget how also to think like human beings. Because for all its rigorous standards and exacting procedures, the practice of medicine is a deeply personal and human endeavor. It is a delicate and demanding art at the end of which, when well-practiced, is renewed life and freedom from suffering and fear for our patients.

I also hope we will identify ourselves after today not *only* as doctors, but also as activists, peacemakers, states-people, ambassadors, innovators, philosophers, or engineers. Moreover, I hope we will identify as artists, continually pushing the limits of our imagination, expanding the boundaries of our dreams about what good medicine can do.

My fellow graduates, look to your left. Now look to your right. Each of those incredible people is a doctor. Sonia and I shared the dream that all of us are fulfilling here today. And while she cannot be here with us in person to revel in our shared achievement, I believe we're only here because it's a dream she, I . . . *we* shared. Today and from now on we are doctors because we did this *together*.

· · ·

JUNE 16, 2014, HONG KONG

Random weekend layover. A fortnight ago I was back home, celebrating together with loved ones over pomp and circumstance. But now I float aimlessly among unfamiliar homes away from home.

Where am I? Who am I?

The wanderer is alone. He is but a single leaf drifting in a forest, relishing anonymity granted by the countless cities that shelter him.

He will lose himself dancing among the spices of endless food and the flickering lights of faceless buildings before him.

But perhaps by choice or perhaps by destiny, the wanderer will learn: Solitude is but another transient state of existence; the world will find him somehow.

And with each discovery, with every human connection he nurtures from a lonely twilight to the birth of another dawn, with every first goodbye before his next flight, the wanderer will arrive a step closer to whatever he is searching for.

CYTOKINE STORM

~~~~~~

April 16–30, 2020

n. (sī·*tuh*·kīn storm) an overreaction of the
immune system, in which an excess of proteins
triggers an onslaught of white blood cells,
resulting in inflammation, possible tissue
damage, and in extreme cases, organ failure.

APRIL 16, 2020

We are halfway through April and I still wonder out loud every day if we are now another step closer to progress or desperation. My brother sends me a video of a mutual friend "disinfecting" an N95 mask for thirty minutes in a 70°C (158°F) sous vide bath. Microwaves to sous vide. Everyone needs a hobby.

Since everyone has gotten into baking or buying new knife sets as if we all became lockdown chefs, what's next? Putting masks in toaster ovens? Cutting out soiled parts of the mask?

It's like when I ate around the mold to save money on bread back in college.

"I did not observe any degradation of the mask after the thirty-minute cook," he earnestly reports. "Hopefully this method can help people get a bit more mileage out of the masks we have." This is what we've come to.

And this headline is why:

Santa Monica Nurses Suspended for Refusing COVID-19 Care Without N95 Mask[1]

Providers in every part of the country are still expected to put themselves at extraordinary—and unnecessary, if administrators and officials had been even minimally prepared—risk. So now we're left sharing sous vide recipes to keep our jobs and to stay alive.

I start a shift in Queens at noon and notice new alerts on the intercom: The Beatles sing "Here Comes the Sun" each time an intubated COVID-19 patient upstairs improves enough to have their breathing tube removed so they can breathe on their own. So far today I've heard the song twice and an overhead page to help with a code once. That symbolizes "two steps forward, one step back," right? One can dare to daydream even within nightmares.

Healthcare workers from around the city message me as well to report the songs their hospital systems are spinning. "Here Comes the Sun" appears to be the favorite, but Journey's "Don't Stop Believin'" and Alicia Keys and Jay-Z's "Empire State of Mind" are also getting airtime. (All three are solid choices. Well done, NYC.)

EMTs now bring in an eighty-year-old patient who had tripped and fallen, and I diagnose an intercranial brain bleed on the CT scan. After an hour of trying to track down a neurosurgeon, the clerk pages me back: "Sorry for the delay, Dr. Sun, they're telling me either the neurologist or the neurosurgeon on call today just died last Sunday from COVID-19."

What the fuck?

After an awkward pause and a stammered "Oh my goodness," the clerk reassures me she will look for backup neurologists and neurosurgeons from other hospitals. She eventually locates one an hour later who can take my patient, and the eighty-year-old is on her way to Manhattan five minutes thereafter.

A few minutes later a doctor at Elmhurst messages to ask if I can take a few minutes to FaceTime—*oh no*—with my grandfather, even though his oxygen mask will probably make it a silent film. How can I say no?

He's sitting upright and his face is animated. He waves and shoots a quick thumbs-up. I wave back and flash him the shaka sign. His medical team tells me he has improved enough to head home soon, and I feel suddenly relieved. I thank them and get back to work, hoping the next time I talk to him he'll be at home and able to talk back. *Maybe able to do more than hand gestures over FaceTime. Maybe a hug.*

A colleague from residency texts me a photo of a patient he's treating: "Notice anything crazy?" She appears young, maybe in her thirties, though I can't see her face. I notice she's on oxygen, but at the same time she's sprawled comfortably on her stomach to use her phone, looking more like she should be on a beach sunbathing than in an ER bathing in supplemental oxygen.

My eyes dart around the picture for clues and finally catch sight of the pulse oximeter level that measures the oxygen in her blood: 54 percent! That's a number that, on any day before COVID, we would consider incompatible with life. Yet here she is, resting comfortably and scrolling on her phone, because the physics of proning opens up parts of the lungs that might otherwise stop inflating.

That's when it hits me: The absence of symptoms we would expect with hypoxia (a low level of oxygen in the body) is a big reason some COVID-positive patients wait until it's too late to seek treatment. Without those big red flags—shortness of breath, wheezing, confusion, racing or palpitating heart, bluish skin—nobody knows they're in immediate danger until the danger is already busting down the door.

This all-too-frequent phenomenon associated with COVID will soon be given a name: "silent hypoxia." Patients appear well one minute, then suddenly collapse into respiratory failure and cardiac arrest.

Now that we've weathered the first wave of infections, we have to switch gears. Rather than reflexively warning healthy-seeming people away from our ERs, we need to give them tools to effectively assess if and when they should go—otherwise they may wait too long. This back-and-forth messaging is exhausting to both sides of the message and feels unforgiving.

I post my musings on social media and soon have a crowd-sourced list of instructions (in multiple languages!) from providers who have all been thinking along the same lines. The biggest takeaway: *Got COVID? Don't lie down on your back.*

○ ○ ○

If You Are to Ever Contract or Are High Risk for COVID-19:
If you or anyone you know are diagnosed with COVID-19 but still feel well enough to stay home (so as not to spread the virus to others), become more aggressive with the following:

1. Engage in safe physical activity (such as walking around the house, proning yourself on your stomach) to help you breathe better and prevent possible clot formation.

2. Coordinate closely with a primary care doctor via Telehealth/Skype/Zoom/FaceTime (messaging a doctor via casual social media like myself **DOES NOT COUNT**).

3. Monitor symptoms with a verified **pulse oximeter ("pulse ox")** device, whether mailed over by an online purchase, the primary doctor, a local healthcare facility, and even some ERs. (For the record, smart phone apps are **not as good** as they measure only one waveform, not multiple, and thus may add another unnecessary risk).

Check your oxygen levels by placing the pulse ox on the middle or index finger of your dominant hand. If you have COVID-19 and your fingers do not have any known circulation problems, are not cold, not sporting nail polish, and the device shows a legit SpO2% value **less than 88–92%** (the exact threshold depends on your medical history and the doctor you choose to coordinate with) consistently for more than 5 minutes, call your doctor. You may have to go to the ER **immediately** for supplemental oxygen to prevent the worst outcomes of silent hypoxia.

To tackle BOTH the challenge of avoiding the virus' contagiousness and yet also preventing the newly observed phenomenon of silent hypoxia, we must act neither too early nor too late.

If You Don't Have COVID-19: When Can We Go Out/Travel Again?

IF YOU ARE WELL/STILL DO NOT have COVID-19 or symptoms: I suggest that you not worry about silent hypoxia just yet. Instead, it may be more productive to fortify your baseline mental health and take control of your life again.

Watch the numbers in your area when things start opening up—if they stay consistently low after 2–3 weeks (the average incubation time it takes from exposure to symptoms), then that could be your cue to take the next step toward restarting your life, depending on your risk tolerance and personal circumstances. If you do decide to take a step outside, continue to proceed with caution: Maintain elevated hygiene standards (wash your hands with soap & water, wear a mask, etc.), be aware of touching others, keep clear of crowds, and avoid small tightly packed interiors with minimal air flow. In other words: Always look out for the safety of yourself and others.

But if numbers spike up after 2–3 weeks, then you know we're not yet in the clear, that the virus does not care about the weather, and you had a 2–3 week head start with staying inside and safe from exposure.

APRIL 17, 2020

Today's hospital doesn't have much of a changing area and stripping down outside in broad daylight would be extra even for me. So I don my PPE in the hallway of an apartment that's been deserted for weeks now. Ah, freedom.

I'm trying DuoDERM for the first time in an attempt to protect my savaged face and hands from twelve to sixteen more hours in PPE. Right out of the gate it seems like an improvement from Band-Aids, so I feel optimistic. I guess we'll see! Check with me fourteen hours from now . . .

By early afternoon we've had only thirteen patients in this ER, ten of them positive for COVID-19. That's certainly a massive improvement over our high of seventy to seventy-five per day just a couple of weeks ago. The lockdown truly at least has performed on its main job: preventing our ERs from collapsing.

Around 2:00 p.m. I get a text from Elmhurst letting me know my grandfather's oxygen saturation has begun to drop into the seventies. *No no no no no no no no no no no no no.* I reply and ask them to prone him immediately.

A few minutes later: "Thanks, proned him with some success! 95% oxygen on his right."

I feel a small measure of relief but don't like the direction toward which he's headed. I take a short break outside for a mental and physical breather, but just then an ambulance arrives and the EMT hands me an EKG of a patient clearly in the middle of an acute heart attack. *No breather for me.* I sprint inside, initiate anticoagulation through his IV, finish the resuscitation, and get him reloaded in the ambulance for transport to the nearest cardiac catheterization lab.

That's when I realize my mask was off the entire time. The attempted breather I had tried to give myself outside may have just killed me.

I almost throw up my hands again in defeat, but right there next to me in the EMS bay I catch sight of a giant negative filtration system. *Can I really be this lucky? The one time I forget to put on my mask there's actually filtered air? Crazy.*

I leave work under a sudden rainstorm tonight as if I were in a monsoon, and I'm glad. Vibrations from the brontide feels like a hug from nature. Pulses and breaths: I still have both.

Whoever said only sunshine brings happiness has never danced in the rain.

Also, DuoDERM has been a big step up from Band-Aids to prevent blistering.

Hurricane droplets.

They lap softly against your face as you slumber half-conscious through a taxi ride on a bridge of a city you still feel as if you hardly know. I channel bliss in my solitude. As city lights flicker across the rim of a half-open window, adorning the invisible grace of a summer night sky, your hair resigns itself to reckless winds. Time loses all meaning in this languid twilight, as thoughts of tomorrow and tomorrow's tomorrow soon render themselves into oblivion.

Seven weeks ago, doubt and ambiguity engulfed my sentences. But once more I glance at these city lights that I almost had forgotten, recalling how I nearly felt at home on this unfamiliar terra firma.

Seven weeks ago, life was different.

APRIL 18, 2020

I'll be one of the very first people to get a COVID-19 antibodies test—today!—and I'm stoked. I'd like to know if I've had this damned disease and just never had symptoms. If so, I can be a donor for convalescent plasma. That'd be cool.

If I do *not* have antibodies, there seem to be four reasonable possibilities, not all equally plausible:

1. I have managed not to catch the virus.
2. I caught it but didn't get symptomatic enough to mount an immune response.
3. I have acquired immunity from eating off the floor in airports.
4. I have natural immunity like Matt Damon's character in *Contagion*.

A snap poll of my social media followers has 78 percent for Matt Damon and some kind of natural immunity, 22 percent for some kind of acquired immunity from being a dirty, dirty man. But maybe most of them just are Matt Damon fans.

And if I'm positive for antibodies? Forgive my trust issues, but I resolve to continue wearing PPE. We don't know yet if testing positive for serological antibodies is evidence for immunity against reinfection—especially if there end up being significant mutations. It's possible to get the flu or a cold every year, and people need occasional boosters for tetanus, polio, and typhoid. With COVID-19, anything is possible: This virus is too new and too weird for me to go into work, or to any other hotspot, without all the protection I can muster.

So at least at this point, the only potential clinical impact of testing positive will be my ability to donate plasma. And maybe just a little less anxiety. That'd be cool too.

APRIL 19, 2020

I scroll through today's headlines and see that three colleagues from three different hospitals are pulling back the curtain to share their day-to-day experiences on the frontlines. Thank goodness they're getting some media coverage too; people need to know what it's like for us. And we need to know we're not in this alone.

An emergency medicine professor at Columbia published an op-ed in the *Atlantic* yesterday. He writes powerfully about healthcare workers' sense that we're on our own, without institutional or government support:

> There has been an abdication of leadership at the highest levels of this crisis that has trickled down to me, a physician in an ER with inadequate personal protections telling oxygen-starved patients to come back when they cannot speak a full sentence or are coughing up more than one tablespoon of blood. These institutions . . . are teaching me a lesson through absence: how to manage a pandemic alone.[2]

But the truth is, we're not the only ones suffering the fallout. My friend and NP colleague named Grace, who moved over to pediatrics from emergency medicine before the pandemic, messages me about what she's seeing:

○ ○ ○

The behavioral health component in children right now is shocking. Those with OCD, autism, aggression who require structure and had routine in school and afterschool programs are now coming in requiring immediate meds and even restraints because of how poorly they are coping. That "fourth wave" is going to be rough.

Her message reminds me to consider the silence of those who cannot bear to counsel or be counseled, the aftereffects of a generational trauma that none of us have ever experienced before. I fear for the wave of self-harm and injury. Perhaps they want to regain some semblance of control they've lost during the prime years of their lives. A life cut short in response to living cut short. Children and adults. Colleagues. I shudder at the thought.

Now that we have the time to think of these things, this respite feels less and less like one with every waking moment.

I shake my head. Now that the initial onslaught has receded somewhat, it feels like a lot of us are contemplating what's outside the bubble, both in our surroundings and our inner lives. Up on my building's modest five-story roof, I try to distract myself from a worrisome, uncertain future by focusing on the present. What I can control for now, at least. So I gaze across the city and my mind drifts toward the alternative to self-destruction: self-affirmation, actualization, love. And nothing feels as relevant to my identity right now as the city I've called home for the past thirty-three years. An identity as a New Yorker. A city I love.

It's been years since I've been home for this long of an uninterrupted stretch. Any situation would feel more dire when a bird clips its own wings. I miss monsooning. My vivid lockdown dreams filled with *Fernweh* have been of monsooning, but lately instead of taking place in a foreign country, they're set in my home city.

Is this city my identity?
Or just a childhood memory
Soon forgotten when I take off.
Like an indifferent adolescent,
Impatient for his independence, a life to claim as his own.

Will I miss the city then?
Ride the subways, span the tunnels—
The unlimited energy of the New Yorker.
Lower East pub crawler, Upper West pupil,
A patron of Washington to Brooklyn Heights.
SoHo shopper, Chelsea bar hopper, Tribeca filmmaker,
Multiple personalities lace together multiple districts.
But shouldn't I have one identity
To call my own?

One distinction with which I am comfortable
To come home the same person as when I left
Or else be without an identity.

APRIL 20, 2020

I now arrange my precious PPE to be right outside my door for easy on, easy off in the hallway—like the Iron Man suit assembly line at Stark Tower. (I stubbornly believe my rich fantasy life is beneficial, therapeutically speaking. If the antibodies test comes back negative, maybe I'll chalk it up to manifesting my superhero visions.)

I'm not aware of any official change in the state's stay-at-home order, but traffic in Manhattan is heavier today than it has been in weeks. Related or not, I also see ten COVID-positive patients in the first hour of my shift. By late afternoon, I post today's stats and ask to hear from other NYC providers on what they're seeing.

- It's busier again: volumes increasing to pre-COVID levels with more non-COVID complaints
- A bounce in ER visits seems likely this whole week: Patients who have followed the lockdown protocol are desperate enough for care that they're willing to take the risk of COVID-19 exposure.
- Upstairs beds are still full. I've transferred 13 admitted patients to other hospitals because we have no beds here.
- First ER COVID-19 death in several days. Hoping this is a one-off and not the start of a trend.

A few minutes later responses start rolling in:

○ ○ ○

[From an EMT:] Yes, it's getting busier. :-(Was hoping things were getting better, apparently not, we're getting huge call volume again for cardiac arrests.

[From a colleague in Staten Island:] My cousin is an intern at RUMC, she has patients waiting >115 hours in the ED for a bed, even tho their COVID load has lightened.

[From another colleague, this one at RUMC:] I'm at the same hospital. It's because patients in upstairs beds are vented and can't get off, so we're just waiting for them to die or recover. We're not getting a bunch of new patients but at the same time we're not getting any more beds.

[From a med school classmate in Brooklyn:] Lots of non-COVID emergencies. Severe diabetic ketoacidosis and strokes.

[From an ER in a higher-income Manhattan neighborhood:] Today sucks and so did last Friday. I thought this shit was getting better. Guess I was wrong. Increase in volumes, and our covid patients aren't doing well all of a sudden. I don't understand it! We were doing so well.

[From a nurse in the Bronx:] Yuuppp same at Jacobi.

It's a different kind of moral injury when we all want to be wrong.

APRIL 21, 2020

Different ER in a different borough today at 7:00 a.m. Let's find out if yesterday was isolated or the start of a citywide surge.

By 10:00 a.m. I've intubated a COVID-19 patient for the first time in a couple of weeks, but overall patient count remains low. The truly sick ones are coming in a trickle instead of a deluge.

A friend in Queens texts a video of people in bunny suits carrying a stretcher bearing a covered body from an apartment building. Dead bodies at home instead of in the hospital.

It's pouring again, so I take my lunch under a canopy by a refrigerated truck that doubles as this hospital's morgue annex. A small tear in the plastic canvas above me suddenly widens and water gushes through, just missing me and my plate of food. It's hard not to see omens everywhere.

APRIL 22, 2020

I start my morning with some light reading on the 1918 flu pandemic:

> Besides replicating very quickly, the 1918 strain [of H1N1] seems to trigger a particularly intense response from the immune system, including a "cytokine storm"—the rapid release of immune cells and inflammatory molecules. Although a robust immune response should help us fight infection, an over-reaction of this kind can overload the body, leading to severe inflammation and a build-up of fluid

in the lungs that could increase the chance of secondary infections.[3]

I've heard repeatedly over the past few days from my grandfather's medical team at Elmhurst. He has continued to take off his oxygen mask when no one is looking "because it's annoying me," causing his saturation levels to drop and putting him at increased risk for organ failure. The team has tried to keep him calm with a mix of mental health counseling and antianxiety medication, and he's starting to show slight improvement.

Given the pattern I've personally seen play out in so many other patients, his creeping re-improvement hasn't been reassuring. I want to see clear, measurable recovery and a massive drop in his viral load. Until then I'm afraid to celebrate.

I also finally receive my antibodies result: negative.

What?? Not going to lie, I'm surprised and a little disappointed. Setting aside the very real possibility that this test is unreliable crap, a positive result might have given me some measure of relief, knowing my immune system had already faced down the virus and come out on top. On the other hand, I would have felt guilty for (unknowingly) exposing so many of my patients.

I guess it's another moral injury when there's no right way to feel.

APRIL 23, 2020

My grandfather died last night.

As with so many COVID-19 patients who seem to get better before they get worse, he got worse.

My grandfather died last night.

The ongoing pressure of supplemental oxygen caused one of his eighty-six-year-old lungs to pop like a balloon and collapse. His medical team then induced him into a coma so surgeons could insert a plastic tube in his chest and suck out the leaked air, as well as to allow for his collapsed lung to reinflate. The procedure seemed to be a success.

My grandfather died last night.

Things were looking up, but then his platelets level began to drop: Thrombocytopenia—one of the measures we use to predict a poor outcome. They phoned for consent to transfuse platelets and my grandmother gave the go-ahead on my advice. But then hours passed, and, even though they had eased up on sedation, he didn't wake up. They tried to take him for a CT head scan to rule out brain bleeding, but during transport he became hypoxic and went into shock. Just as I would have done, his team called the code and began CPR. But to no avail.

My grandfather died last night.

He is gone.

APRIL 26, 2020

My grandmother seems to want to follow after my grandfather as she calls me crying in his absence, saying she has a fever now and wondering if she can head to the same hospital to be closer to him. I tell her no.

She also now has COVID-19 symptoms herself but this time she listens to me and, so far, is able to quickly change her mind and agrees to stay home. I remind her again every time we speak among her wails of her loss: Stay. Home.

In the stupor of early mornings, I suddenly gasp aloud in grief. *Why didn't he listen to my pleas to stay home? Even if he still had died, at least it would have been in a familiar bed with his wife holding his hand, instead of staring at an unfamiliar ceiling surrounded by faceless strangers.*

I dig out a poem my best friend Lei wrote fourteen years ago for my father's funeral. There is strange reassurance in reminding yourself that some questions don't have an answer; perhaps half the battle is summoning up the strength to even show up and ask them.

> Raise your eyes skyward:
> tunnels of light, grains of sand.
> Pardon, for they know not
> the questions and answers we advance.
> Neither are words sufficient
> nor sighs to commemorate and summon
> those who can no longer listen.[4]

APRIL 27, 2020

My grandmother reports she is starting to feel better—physically, that is. She's still a crying mess when we FaceTime. It's weirdly encouraging because her cries make it easy to tell she's not short of breath.

The ER I walk into today is empty. I last worked here on March 26, and we saw 186 patients in twenty-four hours. Now we're averaging fewer than half that number on the board, including:

Bug stuck in ear
Popcorn stuck in nose
Removal of stitches

And yet I am beginning to pick up on my own physical and mental slowness and self-diagnose crisis fatigue. I guess a death in my family, coming on top of the past two months, was the parabolic straw on the allegorical camel's back. Don't want to stay, can't go anywhere. *I don't want to be here, I don't want to be anywhere.*

I'm also hearing that hospital administrations are preparing to cut shifts and staff members across the city's ERs. I'm sure I'm not the only per diem who needs and will appreciate a mandatory break, but I worry about the regular full-time employees. I find myself praying that the people who stepped up in this unimaginable crisis don't get kicked to the curb now that the worst has apparently passed.

Somehow, I know that prayer will go unanswered.

APRIL 28, 2020

I received news this morning that one of my favorite head nurses in Brooklyn, Maria, has died from COVID-19. She was my friend. I remember working with her as a medical student from 2010 to 2014 and then as an attending for the past two years. She said she remembered me when I returned. She teased me. She patted me on the back. She told good jokes. She held me, and so many others, to incredibly high standards. She looked out for me. She looked out for all of us.

We were supposed to look out for her too.

All too familiar tears swell yet again. I feel crushed. *How many more?*

Before long I have two headlines for an answer:

Top E.R. Doctor Who Treated Virus Patients Dies by Suicide

"She tried to do her job, and it killed her," said the father of Dr. Lorna M. Breen, who worked at a Manhattan hospital hit hard by the coronavirus outbreak.[5]

~~~

New York City EMT Dies by Apparent Suicide at 23 Amid Coronavirus Pandemic

John Mondello was found dead near Astoria Park on Friday, according to police.[6]

I need to step away, to take a break, not because I'm already burnt-out, but so I *don't* burn out and sustain moral injury. I hand over my social media to my epidemiologist friend and fellow monsooner Diana, who agrees to take over for a couple of days. We don't have to go through this alone.

APRIL 30, 2020

Two more signs that our city's overall prognosis may be improving, considering the circumstances. First, EMS is reimplementing pre-COVID protocols for cardiac arrest. (Patients in acute cardiac distress can now expect to get immediate medical care again!) And second, the good ship USNS *Comfort* has unmoored from Pier 90 and is steaming her way back to Norfolk, Virginia, after treating a grand total of 182 COVID-19 patients during her one month with us.[7] *Bon voyage, bonne chance.*

Whether I'm in mourning or just because it's overgrown, I cut my own hair for the first time ever. I blast Avril Lavigne's "Sk8er Boi" for inspo and post not-terrible before and after pics on social media. Shortly thereafter a friend tags me in a throwback to a trip to South Africa in 2016 when my hair had been equally short. How I miss being on a plane! How I miss the perspective of home I gain when I'm away from it.

For now I will still follow my own advice: Stay. Home.

As infection and death rates drop, our ERs begin to empty out, and so many colleagues are being furloughed or losing livelihoods. I try to reframe for myself this forced sabbatical.

I want to paint the skies orange red
capture the chemiluminescence of an idea long gone.
I want to journey beneath the surface of the moon

and reflect the rays of a garish sun.
I want to weave together the threads of disproportionate
    reality
dreams manifesting, long buried under miles of doubt.
The music flying low, floating through, knowing everything.

For now I'll begin to explore my hometown with fresh eyes. Every time I step outside for a walk in this near-empty city, I take a breath of hope for renewal as if I were celebrating a birthday. April showers continue to wash away the detritus of our sins and every waking moment is an opportunity for redemption.

13 YEARS AGO

~~~~~~

Spring 2007 / Spring 2020: Jekyll & Hyde

Today is my dad's birthday and the eight-month mark since he passed away. It feels like years and it feels like days.

Beside me is a cake I eat alone for him. I'm at home and my mother is sleeping as I type this into digital oblivion. All is dark except for a computer screen and the backyard lights my mom leaves on so she doesn't feel alone. Contrary as ever, I value solitude. Self-reflection feels urgent, a necessity.

I live in two worlds, as two people: the consummate showman and the introspective observer. It's a stable dichotomy, a cherished (often unacknowledged) hypocrisy. Long have I existed in this paradox. Obliviousness and self-consciousness hold hands like lovers, never arguing, always compromising and complementing one another.

I live in two worlds, perpetually building and collapsing on each other.

Lately there has been an increasing crush of people clamoring to see the hidden half, shielded as it is by the spectacle of its brasher, flashier opposite. The pressure on my outer defenses grows—the pressure of genuine care and concern, I want to believe, but who knows? And at what cost: perpetuating a lifetime of longing for validation, or a step toward self-revelation? At least this shell-like cartoon character persona and its hard exterior proves an effective filter, trapping those who won't put in the work of understanding beyond being entertained.

. . .

I wrote the paragraphs above nearly thirteen years ago. Reflecting on them now, I'm struck both by how things change and how they stay the same.

Change: I might be a better writer now.

Same: I can be so dramatic and therefore still trying not to take myself as seriously as ever.

Same: I feel just as dichotomous or bifurcated in my identity today as I did as a college sophomore.

Change: I'm more often at peace living in two disparate, diametrically opposed worlds as if I were the two sides of a single piece of paper. Mr. Hyde *is* Dr. Jekyll. The Hulk *is* Dr. Bruce Banner. Dr. Strange the Sorcerer Supreme *is* the surgeon who lost the use of his hands after a sudden accident.

(It's interesting to notice, right now as I write, that some of our culture's most famous alter egos are doctors. Probably coincidence. Or it could be the familiar literary rhyme of being human?)

Every action has its equal, opposite reaction. As in Newtonian physics, so is the human experience. In *my* human experience, at least.

The traumatic loss of my parents—my father to sudden death and my mother to the slow debilitation of Parkinson's disease—catapulted me into life-giving adult friendships and healthy self-reliance. I lost one family and gained another. (To go hard on the Marvel metaphor: I may not be able to perform surgery any-more, but what about becoming the Sorcerer Supreme?)

Without "extreme" travel habits of monsooning that soon fol-lowed thereafter—saving up to take an international trip every month or so, instead of starving myself by saving it for one long binge that may never even happen—it's hard to imagine having survived the extreme demands of medical school. Each extreme lit a fire under my ass for the other, like a seesaw or tug-of-war that cannot work without an equal and opposing force. (One was the Hulk, the other Bruce Banner.)

As I try to make sense of the past two months, I see the same Newtonian dynamic in operation. The "extreme" choice I made to remain per diem, beholden to no single hospital system but also minus the safety net of full-time employment, gave me opportu-nity both to work like crazy (because ironically I was free to choose *not* to) and to speak and write honestly about my experience (with-out having to clear every word with HR).

I've been baring my soul on the tacky nude beach of the internet for seventeen years now, the introspective observer habitually stripping down to have his say, stuttering over mixed similes and fumbling fruitless metaphors, grasping after words that never ex-isted to *literize* and *typeize* my feelings. Writing in public has often felt pointless and self-indulgent. Hell, it's probably *been* pointless and self-indulgent, more often than I'd like to admit.

Yet it's undeniable to me, here on this side of March and April 2020, that my long habit of "extreme" internet oversharing uniquely prepared me to serve my colleagues through an extreme crisis by amplifying our voices, affirming experiences, and connecting our-selves with each other and the wider world.

Without the long-dead Mr. Hyde of my LiveJournal/Myspace/Xanga diaspora, some of us Dr. Jekylls would have shouted into an uncaring, unhearing pandemic void. (I agree, this is now becoming a metaphor stretched too far. I should have quit while I was ahead. Will my editors keep this part?)

My point, I think, is that I will no longer fear letting the introspective observer out to play and make new friends, melodramatic and over-serious as he may be. Or, at least, I will embrace that fear as my lifelong friend as we run together toward the fires of vulnerability and self-disclosure.

Come here, old friend.

CONVALESCENCE

~~~~~~~~

May 1–July 4, 2020

n. (*kon·vuh·les·uhns*) the gradual recovery
of health and strength after illness.

MAY 1, 2020

Dear Dr. Sun,

The letter serves as notification that we are not
reappointing you as per diem staff within the Department of
Emergency Medicine effective as of June 30th, 2020. Based
on our current staffing needs, we anticipate that we will be
able to staff our emergency departments with our standing
faculty members and will not be reliant on staffing from
per diem providers.

Thank you for your service to [our] patients. Should
emergency department volumes, and our associated
staffing needs, increase over the coming months, we would
be happy to discuss bringing you back onto our roster of
per diem providers.

Meanwhile, back in the ER, I've been given the go-ahead to order convalescent plasma for a patient positive with COVID-19. I make the call, and within minutes a hematologist comes downstairs to greenlight the order. An hour later, staff from the blood bank sends over two bags of liquid gold and we begin the infusion. Our patient grins ear to ear. She's not just getting plasma. She's getting a transfusion of liquid hope with a side of later hearing the words "you're going home."

The outlook for many of my colleagues is decidedly bleaker, however. The nationwide cancelation of elective surgeries due to the lockdown has led to a massive income shortfall for our hospitals. Some administrators feel that the only way they can stay solvent is to furlough the very staff that had kept them afloat throughout the crisis. I'll be fine, as I've already worked so much at this point that I have accepted it would be time someone told me I should take a break, but what about those with families that depend on them? We're just now to the point where we can start to deal with healthcare provider PTSD, and now you're going to add the trauma of joblessness for those same frontline workers?

I get the financial pressures on all sides, but there is nothing about this that feels right.

MAY 3, 2020

Today as my shifts dry up, I finally join millions of my fellow New Yorkers (and tens, maybe hundreds, of millions of my fellow Americans) in experiencing my own proper lockdown. William, a colleague from residency, stops by to pick up a few of my leftover N95s. I then hang back longer and sit on the stoop as if I were a dealer running out of customers, while soaking up badly needed and long overdue sunlight. I then take a moment to truly take in how empty the streets are in New York City. And for some odd, perplexing, confusing reason, it feels beautiful to me. I can't believe I just noticed it now a whole month after the lockdown started. Was I unable to notice the beauty in things before?

I begin toying with the idea of going for a walk. If I carry my hospital badges with me . . .

I go back inside. Unnecessary risks.

MAY 4, 2020

My grandmother has now fully recovered from COVID-19. I can tell because when I FaceTime with Mom, I can hear her arguing on the phone about which funeral home can receive my grandfather's remains for cremation. So far, she hasn't found one that's available, but at least she's feeling in good enough spirits to be hustling again.

She still has never stepped foot in an ER.

MAY 5, 2020

The funeral home in Queens that accepted my grandfather's body is sending him three hours north to be cremated at a random place in Connecticut. Their backlog is too heavy.

An EMS colleague and medical scribe, Lana, comes by at midnight for a few masks. She gives me a hug. My first in months. It's both a wonderful and strange feeling.

MAY 6, 2020

For the first time in fifty-two years, the NYC subway will experience a system-wide halt between 1:00 a.m. and 5:00 a.m. for regular cleaning. I then read about increasing evidence for multiple strains of SARS-CoV-2. This light at the end of both the literal and figurative tunnel dims a bit.

My second antibodies test comes back negative, just like the first. I'm just not getting this thing.

MAY 7, 2020

I have to ship an Amazon return today. I celebrate ambling the two blocks to and from the post office, then crawl back into my hole. As if my very own neighborhood became an outdoor rehabilitation center, this is the most I ever walked in my city outside of work since the onset of the pandemic. I feel mostly relieved. So much for my habit of traveling internationally at least once a month; even walking now feels like a victory. With a sigh and a laugh, I throw my hands up in the air. *Success.* I want to tell myself, *Get back out there.*

Through numerous degrees of mutual acquaintances and serendipity, the photographer who snapped my picture several weeks ago on April 13, Kareem, sends me the image he captured out of the blue today. I can't stop looking at it—not because it's of me, but because I see all the scars and wrinkles that tell so much of our story. Not only the story that's past, but the part we're still in, too. It makes me think about the souls and innocence lost in every crevice of despair on my face. Each wrinkle a shift, a patient, a loved one, a loss. My grandfather. They shall never grow older. They shall never go away.

MAY 8, 2020

I just floated through five consecutive days off, my first extended break since the pandemic began. After I leave tonight's ER, I don't have another shift scheduled for eleven days. In the Before-Times, this would mean traveling. But no matter how I try to justify it, there is no such thing as ethical travel right now. *I don't want to be here, but I can't go anywhere.* I must find other ways to recharge.

I write. I ponder. I reframe. I practice gratitude that my hometown is easier to explore than most other places. Parts of it are still foreign to me.

Midnight. I step outside. I wonder: *Am I still awake? Am I still dreaming?*

MAY 9, 2020

I feel the rumbling eight stories below.

The subway.

I wonder how early in the morning it is. It's been otherwise so quiet in this city that rubatosis sets in and I can hear my own heart beat beat beat beat. I'm still alive. Pulses and breaths.

I peel one eye open to see a pale blue glow on the wall. If the subway is running it must be at least past 5:00 a.m.

I decide that if I'm awake enough to calculate that much, then the cortisol rush has probably taken over my body and will prevent me from drifting back to sleep.

And yet I stay in bed in a fetal position, clutching my sheets and holding on to the hope that I could sneak in another hour of sleep. My mind wanders back to the beeps and bells of failing mechanical vents again . . . even when I'm not at work, my soul takes me back to the pandemic.

Later that afternoon I thumb through high school scribbles, feeling oh so emo. Life made more sense when it didn't feel so real. I write down my dreams as if I were back in high school again.

Before the pandemic you could find me alone on the steps of the Met, scribbling thoughts in little black books, sentences infused . . . with . . . ridiculous . . . ellipses . . . that . . . just . . . waste . . . space. It's three dots but never four; two only hiccups, and one is one period. When in doubt, use semicolons.

Dramatizing life in desperate pleas to exist; I'm guilty of the crime. Caught red-handed, yes, I was okay with my Sigur Rós.

Your time is up, the piano in your head battles the world's smallest violin for the final minor fifth chord that resolves into a major third . . . of course, this is the soundtrack of your life. You think you're onto something, something that may change the world, or just your world, or just be something you feel deserves a like or two.

With headphones in your ears, the night sky becomes the familiar stage of your next epiphany. But Soulja Boy comes on after Yann Tiersen. Whoops. You were onto something but then "Superman dat hoe" ruined everything. An accident? No, this is reality. Your world just ended. It was the one dot at the end of three. Don't you know that's against the rules? Do your best to scramble back to that Eluvium. And do your best not to end with a corny line . . .

I pass the interminable days of lockdown with mindless ruminations on *How I will do with whatever the elements of time that may justify the peace and redemption that could belong to me.*

What? That sentence doesn't even mean anything.

As I stare at the word salad I just tossed, trying to decipher meaning in the shreds and threads that briefly gave life to my moribund thoughts, generated by a million action potentials across a galaxy of synapses . . .

I *stop.*

I recall stories from others who have gone on sabbaticals after being discharged from a job or routine. Those who would attempt to "do absolutely nothing" with absolute autonomy to think and do whatever they want and without a daily normal to confine or distract them, instead report a sense of paralysis and motionlessness at the event horizon of despair. When even a worldwide pandemic cannot shock meaning into our tribulations, we are left immobile in the face of cosmic apathy.

A man said to the universe:

"Sir, I exist!"

"However," replied the universe,

"The fact has not created in me

A sense of obligation."[1]

Usually whether it's after trauma or loss, returning from an unexpected and transformative adventure, or making a conscious commitment to unlearn everything they've learned (in my case, all of the above), it is by cozying up to oblivion—when we dare to run toward and dabble in the cold fire of nihilism, laughing in its face with pithy poetic diary entries—that we begin to lay a steadfast foundation for conscious belief. Instead of blind pursuit, or being born into blind faith, we journey willingly into the molten core to obliterate unquestioning ignorance and fight for meaning where meaninglessness begins. Call it faith. Call it spirituality. The energy exists beyond my capacity for human words. It is not a label but an action, a fight to render itself meaningful. Besides, if everything were to be truly meaningless, so must be the very belief in meaninglessness.

And even if there is no why, the search for it keeps my interest. Even if today's victory boils down to these feeble sentences. I *choose* to believe: Conjuring significance *is* significant.

MAY 10, 2020

Today I sift through old family photos looking for my grandfather. Instead I find a picture of me, my father, and my great-grandmother sixteen years ago, taken in the Old Town of Shanghai. I don't remember much except there were multiple generations of Suns sitting for a formal portrait and I passed out on her bed after the session because of a brutal hangover from the night before. I remember when she gently placed her hands on me as I began my slumber, smiling as I drifted off.

My great-grandmother passed away during my senior year of college, while I reveled in the chaos of an on-campus night market. I remember volunteering to get pied in the face for a fundraiser. I felt silly when I found out later she had died, a little ashamed that I was playing the fool while she passed out of this world. Did I dishonor her somehow?

I don't believe so, not now.

I have to believe that being really, truly alive—fully present to the challenges and opportunities that present themselves to me each day—does her that great honor. Same with my father.

My great-grandmother survived the Japanese invasion of World War II and lived long enough to see four generations of her family thrive in two of the world's greatest cities. I honor her existence by living.

MAY 13, 2020

My pediatric advanced life support certification is due for renewal, but all the Manhattan offices are closed. My closest option is in Brooklyn, next door to the ol' medical school alma mater. I feel an opportunity for a trip down memory lane coming on.

After I finish the paperwork and receive my recertification, I take a walk. Sinatra's "New York, New York" drifts down the empty streets from an unknown source as the sun melts into evening. Rivers of golden hour and cotton candy skies reflect and refract in the windows of our student dorms.

The maw of the lion seems to be in retreat; the concrete jungle begins to stir.

My city is rested, my city is waking.

MAY 14, 2020

I take another walk today, this time farther out to a neighborhood hub on 86th and Lexington. I dodge crowds like the *Millennium Falcon* dodges asteroids in *The Empire Strikes Back*, not failing to notice street vendors selling masks.

It used to be bootleg sunglasses and pirated DVDs. Now it's N95s. I just hope the masks aren't bootlegged or pirated too.

MAY 15, 2020

New York City Sets Record of 58 Straight Days with No Pedestrian Fatalities

Polly Trottenberg, commissioner of the city's Department of Transportation, noted during testimony before a City Council committee on Tuesday that New York City had gone 58 days without a pedestrian being fatally struck by a vehicle, its longest stretch since 1983, when statistics were first recorded.[2]

MAY 16, 2020

A scheduled visit with Dr. Weiss, medical director for the marathon in New York City, prompts a walk across Central Park to the Upper West Side. Perhaps a virtual call would be easier, but we are both so stir crazy with cabin fever. We decide to meet up outside, figuring that two doctors, both having survived this long, can chance a meeting in the fresh spring breeze with N95s and some responsible physical distance.

I expect a stroll in a sparsely populated park, but find hundreds of people scattered across green lawns—the healthiest looking group of people I've seen in one place since my flight from Angola the first week of March. Lines around the block for public restrooms, children dancing in circles among their kith and kin, masks pulled down for out-door day drinking, which appears to be suddenly legal. I rub my eyes after two months of waking hell: *What alternate universe is this? The Roaring Twenties?*

I'm told this has been going on for two weeks, even as our infection, hospitalization, and death rates continue to plum-met. I feel an epiphany come on the same way Brad Pitt's character realizes in *World War Z* that the zombies choose to infect only healthy people. *Are we finally discovering a weakness? A solid sign the virus doesn't transmit well outdoors?*

I still feel like I'm dodging bullets, wending my careful way through the reveling crowd. But I also feel shy glimmers of hope shimmering to life.

MAY 17, 2020

Armed with fresh infection statistics (still dropping), first-hand experience of yesterday's mass outdoor gathering, and still-unused N95s, I plot my farthest walk yet.

The nightly 7:00 p.m. applause for shift-changing health-care workers is my sendoff, down 3rd Avenue into Midtown, for a quiet pause at the Kobra firefighter mural on 49th Street. Soon I reach a Grand Central Terminal worthy of a postapocalyptic movie: The promenade remains utterly abandoned, even as flashing timetables assure me the empty trains are running on schedule. Fifteen minutes later I stand at the world's empty crossroads, Times Square, like Tom Cruise in the opening scene of *Vanilla Sky*. A bicyclist careens by, breaking my reverie, as tight household knots spill out of cross streets for the golden hour. I return to my old post-college neighborhood—the stretch of 7th Avenue that feels like the middle child between its two better-known siblings of Times Square and Columbus Circle and the very place where I had made and lost a wager to two friends that would lead me to Egypt for the first time. I stay here for a minute to recall the story.

The night begins to set in, so I turn east down Central Park South to 5th Avenue and then home.

If I synchronize my pace with the traffic lights, I can walk without stopping. A tailwind off the East River luckily keeps me company. And so I stride through my life forward and in reverse: They say you can find solace after a loss simply by ambling the streets of New York. So I walk.

I continue to seek comfort in the known. And yet I now want the freedom of an unknown so fiercely, want fate to finally hand over the reins of my life. Now I realize they've been in my hands all along; how will I know what to do with them?

My heart long with longing, I struggle to catch a full breath. I walk down these familiar streets choking on the relief knowing that I am still alive.

MAY 19, 2020

Real-life hair stylists are offering actual, professional haircuts in the OB/GYN room of the ER I'm working today, accepting payments through Venmo to make ends meet. With only three patients in the whole department, the benefits out-weigh the risks. I may be able to clean, sew, and bandage a deep-tissue laceration without looking twice, but I should not be saddled with the responsibility of cutting my own hair.

In the same vein of growing confidence, I'm ditching the bunny suit while keeping the filtered masks. I'm convinced by growing evidence (and personal experience) that this virus doesn't spread by surface contact. With one less thing to worry about on my plate, that's another victory.

MAY 22, 2020

Walked all the way up to the Guggenheim and back this morning. Looking on my city with new eyes, I'm beginning to heal.

MAY 24, 2020

We've reached one hundred thousand (recorded) deaths from COVID-19 in the United States. This country still needs to heal.

MAY 29, 2020

I now brave a visit to my grandmother in Elmhurst, who asked me to help her retrieve my grandfather's remains and close his bank accounts. This woman is a survivor: feisty and goal-oriented. I now know where I get it from.

We take a cab to keep her as safe as possible, and in the middle of a Queens expressway, I spy a memorial flower arrangement tangled in the tattered remains of yellow caution tape. I wonder who, and why.

2 YEARS AGO

~~~~~~~~

Winter 2019

I sometimes question why and how my daily habit of writing these scrolls has been my love letter to life.

When I began a simple travel blog for a summer trip to Southeast Asia and India before I was to begin medical school—much like the premise of *The Motorcycle Diaries*—and during the monsoon season no less (hence the namesake of the blog itself), I had no idea it would go anywhere further than just that. I expected instead to cease posting the day I would return and begin medical school, thinking of even jumping back to my prior online personal blog that was hosted by a service called Xanga.

But a month later, during medical school, I was already burning out and therefore yearning for a reprieve of equally extreme intensity. With the fortuitous arrival of a wedding in San Diego for a weekend and for the sake of my fragile mental health, I left. I returned forty-eight hours later mentally recharged with the curious thought that spontaneous weekend trips may actually be the answer. I blogged about that. A month later, I left again for forty-eight hours, this time for one day in Hong Kong. I blogged about that one too, especially how the roundtrip flight was $600 and I had

budgeted all semester by patronizing events around campus offering and about to throw away leftover free food, saving me a lot
of money with the help of Tupperware.

I returned, left again, returned, left again: North Korea, Guate-
mala and Belize for Thanksgiving weekend, Iran for spring break.
Ukraine and Poland or Spain and Morocco for winter break, Ant-
arctica, Cuba, Palawan, Route 66, Venezuela, the Silk Road, the
Trans-Siberian, the Balkans, Micronations . . . To paraphrase Jyn
Erso's motivational speech from *Rogue One: A Star Wars Story*, every passing day in medical school and residency, I took the next
chance. And the next. On and on until I thought I could win . . . or
when the chances were spent: I failed, I got back in, failed again,
got back up, kept traveling, and kept blogging. A few soon began
to take notice. Hundreds more followed. Ten years, 185 countries
and territories, and countless travel friends and companions
later . . . the rest is history.

There were no lofty ambitions, no plans to make money, "make
it a business," no expectations of "being an entrepreneur." I've remained this hopelessly oblivious Forrest Gump now with this
lovely crowd running next to me, and when asked over and over
why I move, or "how I did it," all I can say in response is the exact
genuine answer that Forrest Gump gave: "I just felt like running."

That's it. Sometimes it's healthy to channel your inner Alan
Watts, stop thinking so much, and "fuck your dreams": They'll
never come true if you try so hard that it becomes disingenuous;
sometimes you just have to let something take on a life of its own.
In fact I would be curious to know what kind of dreams you'd have
if you were already living one.

And soon the travel community took on a life of its own, and I
became surrounded by like-minded explorers who, like me,
sought the serenade in the first cup of coffee in a new city, or the

joy in freedom that comes with the first few hours of every new adventure.

So to them—and everyone else whom I've had the pleasure of running into during the past ten years—I tip my hat and raise my glass.

Because without you I would not have these ten years to look back on.

Because without you I could never be.

> You can't connect the dots looking forward. You
> can only connect them looking backward. So you
> have to trust that the dots will somehow connect
> in your future. You have to trust in something—
> your gut, destiny, life, karma, whatever.
>
> —Steve Jobs

It's been ten years.

Ten years of accidents. Mistakes. Serendipities.

Ten years since I accidentally lost a bet over roundtrip fare to Egypt, which changed my life forever. Ten years of never slowing down and never looking back. Ten years of momentum. Discipline. Spontaneity.

Ten years would see me to 185 countries and territories—70 of them more than once—and hundreds of strangers that have traveled with me because of a small quirky travel blog that I had first started just to let my mom know I was okay. Ten years since accidentally fostering an environment for a bafflingly interconnected international community that to this day is family. Ten years of traveling both far and together. Ten years of serendipity. Synchronicity. Disbelief. Magic.

Ten years since I was inspired to lose another wager to myself, apply to and then barely graduate from medical school. Ten years would mean $200,000 in student debt, countless exams, and never expecting to make it out either alive or sane, never knowing what the next step would be. Ten years engaging in a war of attrition, countless small victories and countless more failures. Breakdowns. Ten years of becoming a medical student, class president, medical resident, doctor, attending, medical captain, chief physician, and clinical professor.

Ten years of imposter syndrome. Cognitive dissonance. Learned helplessness. Endless, boundless doubt. And yet: Privilege. Gratitude.

Ten years of falling in and out of love more times than even the hopeless romantic thirteen-year-old in me would have wanted. Ten years of watching movies like *Before Sunrise*, *Before Sunset*, *Lost in Translation*, *Once*, *Vanilla Sky*, *Her*, *My Blueberry Nights*, *Eternal Sunshine of the Spotless Mind*, and suddenly realizing each and every one of them already may have happened to me.

Ten years of getting to know the girl on the train and then never seeing her again, colliding with loves of my life and the love of my life. Ten years of sensible growth while staying a hopeless romantic. Ten years of stopping to love myself first before being capable of loving others. Ten years of un-possessive, endless, boundless love.

Happy ten years, happy belated birthday to me, and happy ten years—of travel. Of community. Of new families. Of medicine. Of love.

Of gratitude.

· · ·

And today I'm celebrating my ten years of travel back in Egypt where it all began. Today we change nothing of what I had done ten years ago: Everything has been planned to the tee to be exactly the same except that instead of four friends with me ten years ago, I now have eighteen.

Just like ten years prior, we drove over from Tahrir Square to the Bedouin horse stables, where eighteen horses were waiting for us by 5:00 a.m. They quickly assigned each of us to a horse based on preferences for "fast," "slow," "strong," or "small."

Ten years prior, I chose "crazy."

Today I chose "crazy fast."

We quickly befriended our horses and set off into the darkness (obviously any photos I took came out all black).

Ten years ago . . .

. . . with a sound of a whip breaking through the cold air, my life would change forever. Strings in the air as my horse raced off into eternity, and so did my heart, and I held on for dear life. The poor bastard I was sitting on was galloping away as if we were trying to outrun a jaguar: We were outrunning fate. From the sound of crackling pavement to that of rustling sand, I slowly caught on that I was in the middle of the Sahara Desert: just my horse and I in the blind.

The darkness also overwhelmed me; I couldn't see anything but the color black under a cloudy night sky. I'm not sure if I could brag that "I was riding that horse with my eyes closed!" but this was close enough. And I knew in my bones that if I let go for a second, I'd fall and break something: my camera, my limbs, my head, my dignity. So I held tighter. I channeled prior experience on riding mechanical bulls back home. It seemed as though every gallop would be the last thing I would

ever hear. I remember there was a little voice in my head telling me
that I really wasn't in New York anymore (a little slow, a little late).

Then with a high-pitched whistle in front of me I saw a fire burn in
the distance. Shadows in the light of the fire pointed. I turned my head
over my shoulder . . .

Best bet I ever lost.

As we reached the Giza Plateau, dawn began to pierce the night.
The muezzin call to prayer, the *adhan*, began to fill the air around
us. Familiar emotions from ten years ago came back as if stored
like muscle memory. As if I smelled the perfume of a former lover,
read an old letter to myself, or stepped in a room I had grown up
in, I wept. Luckily nobody saw me in the rhapsody of my tears
through the thickness of twilight.

As a new light began to peek above the haze, we got off our
horses to take it all in: a sun rising above, tears rising below, tears
from those very eyes finally landing upon the silhouettes of the

Great Pyramids on the horizon as if they were teardrops themselves on the face of the desert.

We watched as an occasional harras of horses galloped across the plain.

Best bet I ever lost. Ten years later and it still is.

. . . Today we add a new part to my Cairo itinerary from ten years ago. A few hours after returning from the Giza Plateau, the eighteen of us walk through Qarafa (Cairo's "City of the Dead"), where a woman invited us into her garden of tombs, not accepting any tips from us for her hospitality. We take our time here and acknowledge her silent act of kindness with a smile and a nod.

Then making our way to our next stop, I look back to see her shedding a few joyful tears as if she finally felt that her existence was recognized by a vast world that seemed to have long forgotten her.

• • •

Two months later desert gales wash over my naked chest, and my bare feet burrow into the heat of the earth. I breathe in, bathing in moonlight. For a moment I believe I can see the Almighty moving over the face of the sands. A train leaving to collect iron ore continues on without me. Its light dims. My tent rustles in its wake. I see only stars, the desert, and myself as one of the countless grains of stardust and sand embedded within.

I feel a slight night shiver.

L'appel du vide soon dissociates my consciousness, and for a moment I consider a world in which I no longer exist; I forget that there is me. I always consider the folly of giving the self significance when juxtaposed next to oblivion; it would be a futile effort.

The best I can lay claim to a seemingly careless universe is by telling my story.

Ego soon drifts farther away from me, and I then perceive a world that existed long before and was unadulterated by human consciousness. Unless a deus ex machina explicitly declares today what "should be" beautiful, beauty in the objective sense is so transient it might not even exist at all. Especially if human presence is no longer around to perceive it, can anything really be beautiful in the everlasting sense? If we think nebulas are beautiful, then so is the beauty in transience. The Japanese have a phrase for this, *mono no ware*, as do the Portuguese, *saudade*. I feel both simultaneously, as if I would be living a scene out of a collaboration between Wong Kar-wai and Richard Linklater.

Even if I could arrive at an answer, the rest of the universe—or whoever reads this—may not care what I think is beautiful; we're mere grains of sand in this desert. The universe will keep expanding, this world will keep turning, the desert winds will keep blowing, and time will go on all the same.

Yet the mere miracle of human existence proves this nihilism otherwise. The possibility of our relative capacity for self-awareness must afford each and every one of us the right to at least tell our stories and choose to declare what is beautiful and significant. And so within the vast diversity of human consciousness, beauty can emerge out of relevance. Just like the idea that one particular child can be conceived among countless possibilities, we both rise from and yet still become mere grains of sand in the desert. We perpetuate cycles of transience. "Half the battle is showing up." And that is beautiful.

Although in this lifetime we still must communicate thoughts and ideas that form a collective consciousness of this particular reality we all share, the core of each of those thoughts still rests in the power of individual experiences. In this beauty of relevance we therefore learn that, in the ultimate of the infinite, there must be no ultimate binary: no ultimate right and wrong, no ultimate black and white. The world never operated on a binary code of 0s and 1s, and neither should we. Some of us may choose to do so in order to construct moral compasses suitable for the times—which can be meaningful depending on the circumstances—but when we presumptively impose these personal binary codes on others, or worse, the entire world, whatever meaning something had will descend through the infernos of potential harm and ultimate meaninglessness. It would be a futile effort; the ego that dares to force its code on others must one day reckon with its existence to be as fleeting as a single grain of sand in the desert: The world will keep turning, the desert winds will keep blowing, and time will go on all the same.

But if there are those willing to absorb a new code into their lives without solicitation, obligation or expectation, that's a different story.

Half the battle is showing up.

So I want to ask:

Would any of you even *want* this kind of life? *Feel* this kind of life? Dare to peek above the fences this very world has put up for you? (And perhaps they were put up just to test you.)

Because it's not as pretty as you think.

If so, then say goodbye to your former life and those who stood by you, who felt they gave you everything only to feel betrayed when you walked away. To say "so long" to even those who have known you for so long.

If so, then you and I may be cut from the same cloth, filled with *mono no aware* and *saudade* looking over fences, leaving familiarity behind, embracing hurt, and questioning your purpose on this earth for crossing borders . . .

With these experiences you will soon reckon with the stark reality that we and time past still mean nothing but a speck of sand, a stardust speck among the vast, seemingly endless stretches of this world.

And yet, that means everything.

JUNE 5, 2020

After nearly a seemingly endless three-month stretch, yesterday was the first day since March 11 with no confirmed COVID deaths in NYC.

Since we're in phase I of reopening, my hematologist friend Sharon and I organize a drive over state lines to Ramapo, New Jersey, to celebrate many things—the improving outlook on COVID, the better weather, my partner's birthday—with a hike. Just last month Sharon helped me with creating content about how to better understand convalescent plasma; now we're organizing convalescent outdoor activities together. This is progress. I order each car to keep windows down for airflow and organize two carpool groups according to those who have tested negative and those who have had and recovered from COVID-19. We nickname the latter group the Antibuddies, and I honestly kinda feel jealous.

We start our hike and I notice my labored, Darth Vader breathing under my N95, which I've kept on out of concern for others. Even though the odds of outdoor spread are slim to none, I still won't take the chance that my (now sporadic) work could threaten a friend's life. Plus, I consider how many athletes train in high altitude, purposely depriving themselves of oxygen saturation in order to make their blood cells more oxygen-efficient. So I reframe my outlook: I'm now in training. No excuses.

At the end of our uphill climb we can see New York City: a tiny bump of shining buildings on a hill. A tiny bump of infections, lockdowns, deaths, determination, and now protests for racial reckoning long overdue and delinquent justice that will no longer be denied.

It's a tiny bump. A speck of stardust.

It's home. It's everything.

It's all we got.

JUNE 11, 2020

Seven weeks ago, I took a ten-minute walk around my neighborhood on a rare day off from work. No symptoms.

Five weeks ago, I walked two miles to Midtown and back. No symptoms.

For the past two weeks, I've volunteered as a street medic for BLM protests and walked nearly forty miles. No symptoms.

In the past week, I've been to Ramapo for a hike and Lake Hopatcong for an afternoon, both with friends to celebrate birthdays. No symptoms.

Today my brother and I will drive sixty-five miles north to Milford, Connecticut, to bring back some of my father's personal effects. Let's see what happens . . .

JUNE 15, 2020

. . . still no symptoms. Except that of wanderlust.

JUNE 18, 2020

Overheard in New York City: "Bro, you better wear your mask right. *Over* your nose."

"Fuck off and mind your own business. . . . You're right, though. Thanks."

The city is healing.

JUNE 20, 2020

While NYC's phase II of reopening has begun, I'm still in the earliest phase of processing how the world and I have been reshaped by enforced stasis. Not only have I longed for discrete *things* like hanging out, eating out, working out, and traveling, I also mourn the unknown missed connections, lost opportunities, "what could have beens," and the ones that got away. However necessary mass quarantine may have been to public health—and I am firmly convinced it was absolutely necessary—I am not blasé about the very real mental, emotional, and relational consequences we'll be suffering for who knows how long to come.

I am therefore trying to reframe my emergency-then-lockdown narrative as a pilgrimage, an odyssey undertaken to discover and expand my inner foreign territory, rather than as a trauma perpetrated upon me by outside forces. Yes, really bad shit happens. It has happened before and it will happen again, totally beyond our control. And I want to take every single happenstance as an opportunity to choose growth and resilience. To precipitate courage as the solute within fear. I want to live, fully and gratefully, and to *become* what could have been.

> It dwells in the dark recesses of concrete slabs
> that stretch ad infinitum into unfamiliar territory,
> a place I always called home.
> After eighteen years city streets still lie cold before me,
> granting little reprieve to search for the secret
> I once had hidden in twilight summer winds

Summers in New York City—this is my thirty-third—have always functioned as a reprieve from *what* I do, so I can re-examine *why*. For whatever constellation of reasons, I have more me time, more hours in the day just to be, just to think, just to be alive and wonder and wander. By each summer's end I am more at peace with whatever lies ahead on the path. I look forward to the future, uncertain as it always is and will remain.

And yet day by day the city gives and takes away with endless distractions. Gain a dollar, lose a dollar, you are no different than the person you were before. Whether in a gym or a restaurant, whether at work or at home, I throw myself in as many varying circumstances as possible so that life can still seem interesting by the end of the day. And when I wake up the next morning, I still dread formality and routine . . . the familiarity and the sense of static turmoil.

And yet I wake up because it can be Groundhog Day again; I look forward to another chance to try something different this time around, to live a little beyond the last day, so I understand my limits and what lies beyond the last risk I took. Half the battle . . .

I know this summer will be another one to remember; while I understand the folly of even the act of *looking* for answers, trying to understand questions only these lone summer nights can solve, or decrypting the everlasting mystery that is my current existence and attempting to understand all the unusual events—calamities and serendipities—that have defined the person I have and will become, I still look forward to the day when the building mysteries eventually answer themselves.

Serendipity: I now find myself alone on a bus I slipped onto at the last minute, when its arrival at the curb coincided with a sudden summer squall. It takes me directly home without a stop or anyone getting on as if it were my personal chauffeur. Whether by happenstance or by meaning, this will be my answer and my New York state of mind.

JUNE 28, 2020

For weeks I've been posting COVID-related ups and downs from healthcare colleagues outside of NYC, but after sixty days sheltering in place, it's time to peek over the fences and see for myself. My turbulent dreams—this is a widespread phenomenon, apparently—have become even more vivid of late, stoking in me visions of uncrossed desert and undiscovered forest.

With nearly everyone I know already traveling, no ER shifts scheduled for the coming week, and a COVID-resistant cross-country road trip in the works for August, I'm monsooning into trial mode to research how domestic trips can be safe and responsible, without negative impact on other communities (just like monsoons have always sought to be).

We can either choose to let the narrative of the over-worked, overburdened, heroic frontline healthcare worker define us, or we can reclaim some personal agency and re-write the narrative to be our own. Some of us need to know when and how to step back from our fires to reorient perspectives before charging back in. Empty tanks must be refilled. We are not quitting. We are recharging.

So I'll head northeast tomorrow and the following few days, outside the fifty-mile bubble I've holed up in since the last ice age. I look forward to what dreams may come. I look forward to dreams being more than merely dreams.

JUNE 29, 2020

Monday 10:00 a.m., our first stop is in Elmhurst, Queens, to check in again on my grandmother, whose love language is a gift of my grandfather's socks, taken from his closet and given to me.

After teaching her how to use her mobile banking app, we're on the road again by noon, at that point about an hour and a half into Connecticut, currently less than 2 percent positive for COVID-19 and one of only two states (at time of writing) with continually decreasing rates of infection. Checking and rechecking the infection map, the corridor between NYC to Rhode Island via Connecticut remains blue and "zero- to low-risk."

After a quick (outdoor, obviously) lunch near my father's old office in Milford, we drive another twenty minutes north-east, stopping in for a slice of New Haven–style pizza and a stroll around Yale's deserted campus. I recall hearing on a campus tour with my dad that an eccentric architect ordered acid poured down the walls of Harkness Tower to make it look older. (As a medical student, I wore scrubs instead of a short white coat to look like a higher-level resident physician. *I get it.*)

After a thirty-minute amble, we take our final two-hour drive of the day into Rhode Island, also boasting a less-than-2-percent positivity rate for COVID-19 and declining rates. We check into our first hotel in Providence, where management claims nobody has stayed in our room for at least forty-eight hours, allowing enough time for the virus to have dissipated with open windows and good air flow. (They still make us sign a form that frees them from liability if we catch something.)

I figure hotels with operable windows and good airflow are safer than my job, especially as they're expected to be sanitized more often and thoroughly than private homes: Nobody wants a negative Yelp review reporting they came down with COVID-19 after staying a night there. Furthermore, hardly anyone has traveled *anywhere* during the past three months. For my personal risk tolerance, I'd gladly choose a hotel room over any of the ERs I worked in with insufficient PPE.

After a half hour of freshening up, we reunite with my old friends Lei and Maria again, who just so happen to be in Rhode Island at the same time. The last time I saw them was March 20, when they dropped masks off at my place and just *had* to lovingly point out how shell-shocked I looked.

Walking around Federal Hill down to Riverwalk, we reach the New Providence River Pedestrian Bridge. An eerie silence infuses my first evening in a foreign city since lockdown began. I appear shell-shocked again, this time at the deserted scenery of downtown Providence.

"Is it always this empty or is it COVID?" I ask.

"It's always this empty."

Empty New York City streets are ominous, but here it's normal. If there were a perfect place to wake up in the middle of a pandemic after a yearlong coma—like Jim from *28 Days Later* or Rick Grimes from *The Walking Dead*—and not notice anything amiss, it is here. Just as your namesake, thank you, Providence, for being my first new bed after four months at home. It's a great start.

Travel, how I've missed you.

JUNE 30, 2020

The events of 2020 have made me feel as if I've lived through so many lifetimes that when I now wake up under an unfamiliar ceiling in hotel beds across America, I sometimes forget who I am anymore.

We drive to Newport for a gallivant along Cliff Walk, where American Gilded Age "summer cottages" face the sea. But these are not cottages; they are palaces. I imagine various Vanderbilts quarantining quite comfortably through the 1918 flu pandemic, then remember families I saw in ERs in the outer boroughs during the first COVID wave: Parents with six kids, one or two positive for COVID-19, living together in government-assisted shoeboxes, wincing when I told them "everyone" absolutely had to stay home. In a Manhattan ER the next day, I'd see couples who own three-bedroom apartments and have access to an in-law's cottage in the Hamptons or upstate cabin to escape the city.

Pandemics don't only create new problems. They also highlight age-old disparities.

JULY 1, 2020

We press on to my first time ever setting foot in Maine, where I recall learning how in the early days of our nation's birth, early settlers here considered the ubiquitous lobster as "trash food" and their prisoners would complain about constant lobster dinners constituting as "cruel and unusual punishment."

One era's trash is another one's treasure.

We arrive at a downtown Portland hotel that is reopening today after nearly a month of complete vacancies. (This means our room will definitely be clear of COVID-19, since that's more than enough time for a lonely virus to die alone; as bad as COVID-19 may be, it isn't bedbugs.)

Reception makes us check off and sign a piece of paper without bothering to ask for proof of a negative COVID-19 test. The form requires us to "promise" that we

- have received a negative test result for COVID-19 on a specimen taken no longer than seventy-two hours prior to our arrival, consistent with Maine's CDC guidance;
- will quarantine for fourteen days upon arrival in Maine or for the duration of our stay; or

- have completed a fourteen-day quarantine in Maine prior to our stay.

Setting out on foot and passing the Portland Observatory, we trek along the Eastern Promenade Trail, where the Atlantic Ocean bears tidings from Europe and crashes them in waves on the rocks below. We hear the din of traditional waterfront seafood shanties reopening for outdoor and partial indoor dining. We opt for outside. And lobster, obviously.

JULY 2, 2020

Today we visit Portland Head in Cape Elizabeth, the oldest lighthouse in Maine, first lit in 1791. I gaze up and imagine what it would be like to work as a lighthouse keeper. Lonely, I would think. The passage of time would warp and distort as endless disregard encompasses your daily reality—eternal, unending. At the same time, though: restive and tense. Lives literally depend on you to be watchful, on alert, and to act immediately when voyagers are at risk.

Sounds familiar.

As night falls I channel four months of yearning to unleash a primal scream into the void of twilight—four months of suppressed rage, disappointment, loss, anger, dismay, bargaining, shock, grief, depression, confusion, and everything in between. Tonight as the very mighty lands on the roof of America finally liberate us to howl infinitely eastward over the plains, our catharsis has been deafening; it instead has stunned us into silence.

JULY 4, 2020:
THE LIGHT THAT FOLLOWS THE STORM

We've seen lighthouses aplenty on our drive from Portland, past L.L.Bean's giant boot, toward our next stop: Acadia National Park. I feel as if everyone and their mother in New York City has already made a visit here this summer; I guess it's my turn now to be better late than never.

When I look up at the lighthouse on Bass Harbor Head, my scattered post-lockdown musings finally coalesce into another metaphor.

Wuhan, Italy, and New York City were lighthouses, staffed by stalwart keepers desperate to warn the world of looming danger. We hoped and prayed that our urgent flashing signals would save lives, that voyagers in other cities and towns would heed our alarm and turn their ships around.

It's hard to know if our lights made a difference. I'll be honest: No matter how much I've written down, it remains disheartening to hear from colleagues around the nation about overcrowded ERs, maxed-out ICU beds, shortages of ventilators, systems collapsing, and patients dying from lack of resources. It's tempting to tilt-shift our lonely, restive watch as a failure. There have been too many shipwrecks to account for.

But then I think about those same colleagues, from Arizona to Michigan, Florida to Washington, Texas to Minnesota, flashing their own signals like mad, frantic to get someone's, anyone's, attention.

And I know to my bones the failure is not ours. We have shined the light: watchful, on alert, ready to act. We are the light that follows the storm.

Whether or not anyone is looking, we will keep the light on.

JULY 27, 2020

I decided to finally downgrade from my P100 mask to a regular surgical mask today.

And I still have yet to lay my hands on a PAPR.

1 YEAR LATER

~~~~~~~

Fall 2021: Oath-Taking

We sail together on one of Earth's many excellent bodies of water—and yet we are strangers. We exchange furtive glances of *nunchi* across the bow as salt water anoints our faces. I'm not sure we remember how to make friends anymore. I've done one solo international trip (this past May, to the U.S. Virgin Islands) but this is my first international monsoon with this many other real-life humans since the first week of March 2020. I'm out of practice.

The Tyrrhenian Sea is bounded by the islands of Sardinia and Corsica on the west, the Italian Peninsula to the north and east, and Sicily to the south. Its waves are so blue-green they almost hurt my eyes. As stunning as this corner of the world is, however, all I want to look at are the people now free and their hearts full of hunger. I don't know it yet, but we will soon remember the first steps of friendship, and these strangers will dance into my heart as long-lost family.

I am then transported, now finding myself dancing along marble cobblestone streets under soft rain wondering once more if this is real life or a dream, or whether I'm actually time traveling. And then on the last night of this monsoon, I will breathe in the warm mist of a Mediterranean harbor town about to be monsooned upon. This is a place, a moment, safe from the pandemic that has defined and bounded and constrained me for a year and half.

This town, this night, this mist, this rain, this air: ours.

I now sit in front of a beautifully souled former stranger who duets with her ukulele. The night is so quiet, all we hear is music. I wonder what everyone is thinking, as I watch them watching her. Her kind, soft, mellifluous voice vibrates this air and awakens our spirits. Some of us begin to hum and sing along.

Our voices, this music, this communion: ours.

Tears rise hot against the backs of my eyes. I don't want to leave. I don't want to go back. I want to stay right here with these siblings and loved ones, each of them tired and sun-kissed and gloriously alive. I don't want to return to dying and death. I don't want to be confronted again by our failure to protect so many and our failure to atone and make amends for enduring injustice. I don't even want to dream anymore lest my own dreams take me back to the nightmares I used to live. So I beseech both the third and fourth dimensions, *Please, please, please let me stay. I don't want to go back.*

A familiar voice in my head whispers: *So quit. Leave. You will never be able to stop a pandemic. Patients will still die; racism, lies and misinformation will still spread like the virus itself; healthcare workers will continue to be fed to the lion's maw. You are but cannon fodder for a society that needs scapegoats. So save yourselves. Abandon your calling. Forget your oaths. Zoom out into the vastness of time and space, and you will understand how worthless they are.*

No. Within the molten core of that vastness, I have stood at the crossroads of life and death, and it has been my oath and personal code that has compelled me to stand there. To even show up. Half the battle . . .

In purity and according to divine law will I carry out my life and my art. . . . May I always act so as to preserve the finest traditions of my calling and may I long experience the joy of healing those who seek my help. Sworn in love, it has sustained me as it has sustained so many other healers.

But a year and a half of COVID has also shown me that, on its own, an oath may still not be enough. Showing up may still not be enough.

There beside the Tyrrhenian Sea, surrounded by a family I didn't know I was missing, I stop resisting and loosen my grip ever so slightly. I forgive myself for my thoughts, and instead cherish the solace I have rendered through subsequent writings and dreams. The fact I can imagine this future as a possible reality reminds me how I have been generously allowed to be surrounded by loved ones present and past I likely do not deserve. For I'm still outside in the marina, fearing my longing for reassurance from . . . someone, or something . . . that I am not an imposter, that I deserve their love. That I deserve my father's and grandfather's love. That I deserve this future where I will have survived a pandemic.

Like new lovers tangled in their bedsheets fighting the break of dawn, I realize neither traumatic or blissful moments last forever, and thus the die has been cast. As the walls that contain this other-worldly reality begin to crumble around me, I remind myself how this desire for reassurance is also blinding me, complicating my wandering heart of wonder from fully being present in this eternal moment.

Therefore, neither in the spirit of vigorous resistance nor passive resignation, I joyously embrace instead an earnest *acceptance* of all that I cannot predict or change, a commitment which allows for a clearer mind leading to a more direct kind of action.

And with that I release a lifetime of self-doubt in a cloudburst and let insecurity be swept away in a downpour of love. I let go, and I'm let go. I accept and become accepted. I belong.

From this place of belonging, I swear to a new code and oath: I *will* stay. Not here in this harbor town, forever breathing in this musical, magical air. No, this too will become a beautiful memory—a timely present from a kind universe—and thus must stay as one. Nor in another beautiful memory in the future that has yet to happen. Instead, I will stay and find beauty in the presence of *being* present. I will stay really, truly alive. Whether I'm on the frontline fighting through whatever foggy, uncertain future SARS-CoV-2 will share with its variants, or being open, vulnerable, and present on future travels with as-yet unknown monsooners accompanying me for the ride, I will stay. After all, the greatest gift we may bequeath to the future is giving all we can to the present.

The irony strikes me then: An "extreme" kind of travel led me to this moment, when I promise never to leave wherever I find myself.

Whoever I become and wherever I am, there I will *stay*. This I swear.

And with the reins in my hands, "we have a code." A new oath.

I smile, and stay right where I am.

NOTES

Pyrexia

1. Melanie Evans and Khadeeja Safdar, "Hospitals Facing Coronavirus Are Running Out of Masks, Other Key Equipment," *The Wall Street Journal*, March 18, 2020. https://www.wsj.com /articles/hospitals-facing-coronavirus-are-running-out-of-masks -other-key-equipment-11584525604 (accessed September 2021).

Dyspnea

1. Centers for Disease Control and Prevention, "Strategies for Optimizing the Supply of Facemasks," Wayback Machine, March 18, 2020, 21:33:23. https://web.archive.org/web /20200318213323/https://www.cdc.gov/coronavirus/2019-ncov /hcp/ppe-strategy/face-masks.html (accessed October 2021).
2. Centers for Disease Control and Prevention, "Strategies for Optimizing the Supply of Facemasks."
3. Centers for Disease Control and Prevention, "Strategies for Optimizing the Supply of Facemasks."
4. Alex Lubben, "U.S. Hospitals Are Wildly Unprepared to Deal with How Bad the Coronavirus Pandemic Could Get," VICE News, March 19, 2020. https://www.vice.com/en/article/dygejq/us -hospitals-are-wildly-unprepared-to-deal-with-how-bad-the -coronavirus-pandemic-could-get (accessed October 2021).
5. Alice Su, "Doctors and Nurses Fighting Coronavirus in China Die of Both Infection and Fatigue," *Los Angeles Times*, February 25, 2020. https://www.latimes.com/world-nation/story/2020-02-25 /doctors-fighting-coronavirus-in-china-die-of-both-infection-and -fatigue (accessed October 2021).

6. Jack Dolan and Brittney Mejia, "LA County Gives Up on Containing Coronavirus, Tells Doctors to Skip Testing Some Patients," *Los Angeles Times*, March 20, 2020. https://www.latimes.com/california/story/2020-03-20/coronavirus-county-doctors-containment-testing (accessed October 2021).

7. Alison Escalante, "Doctor's Don't Perform Well When They Are Afraid," *Forbes*, March 22, 2020. https://www.forbes.com/sites/alisonescalante/2020/03/22/doctors-dont-perform-well-when-they-are-afraid/?sh=74462fc13592 (accessed October 2021).

8. Heather Willden, "COVID-19: Joint Statement & Guidance Document on Multiple Patients Per Ventilator." American Association for Respiratory Care. https://www.aarc.org/joint-statement-guidance-document-on-multiple-patients-per-ventilator/. March 26, 2020.

Morbidity

1. Ali Watkins, "N.Y.C.'s 911 System Is Overwhelmed. 'I'm Terrified,' a Paramedic Says," *The New York Times*, March 28, updated March 31, 2020. https://www.nytimes.com/2020/03/28/nyregion/nyc-coronavirus-ems.html (accessed October 2021).

2. The Chainsmokers, "New York City." Spotify. https://open.spotify.com/track/4vlCvZazmdpxQLEt3sCeKH.

3. Sophie Tanno, "Woman, 90, Dies from Coronavirus in Belgium . . ." Daily Mail.com, March 31, 2020. https://www.dailymail.co.uk/news/article-8173075/Woman-90-dies-coronavirus-Belgium-refusing-ventilator.html (accessed October 2021).

4. Tom Winter, "NYC Emergency Medical Services . . ." NBCnews.com *Health News* (blog), April 2, 2020. https://www.nbcnews.comhealth/health-news/live-blog/2020-04-02-coronavirus-news-n1174651/ncrd1175016#blogHeader (accessed October 2021).

5. Dylan Scott, "New York Is Merging . . ." Vox.com, April 3, 2020. https://www.vox.com/2020/4/3/21207310/coronavirus-new-york-hospitals-andrew-cuomo (accessed October 2021).

6. Governor Andrew Cuomo (@NYGovCuomo). 2020. "#BREAKING: I spoke to the president and he has agreed to our request to treat #COVID patients on the USNS Comfort." April 6, 2020, 5:29 p.m., https://twitter.com/nygovcuomo/status/1247275243321737216

7. Josh Farkas, "PulmCrit Wee: Could the Best Mode of Noninvasive Support for COVID-19 Be . . . CPAP?" EmCrit.org, March 17, 2020. https://emcrit.org/pulmcrit/cpap-covid/ (accessed October 2021).

8. Gwynne Hogan, "Staggering Surge of NYers Dying in Their Homes . . ." Gothamist.com, April 7, 2020. https://gothamist.com /news/surge-number-new-yorkers-dying-home-officials-suspect -undercount-covid-19-related-deaths (accessed November 2021).

9. Phoebe Zhang and Guo Rui, "Coronavirus: Why Many Deaths . . ." *South China Morning Post*, February 12, 2020. https://www.scmp .com/news/china/society/article/3050311/its-pneumonia -everybody-china-knows-about-many-deaths-will-never (accessed November 2021).

10. Rob Quinn, "Some Doctors Are Questioning the Use of Ventilators," Newser.com, April 9, 2020. https://www.newser.com /story/289331/some-doctors-are-questioning-the-use-of -ventilators.html (accessed December 2021).

Cytokine Storm

1. AP, "Santa Monica Nurses Suspended . . ." via KTLA.com, April 15, 2020. https://ktla.com/news/local-news/santa-monica -nurses-suspended-for-refusing-covid-19-care-without-n95-mask/ (accessed December 2021).

2. Stephen McDonald, "No One Is Supporting the Doctors," *The Atlantic*, April 18, 2020. https://www.theatlantic.com/ideas /archive/2020/04/doctors-already-manage-alone/610249/ (accessed December 2021).

3. David Robson, "Why the Flu of 1918 Was So Deadly," BBC Future, October 30, 2018. https://www.bbc.com/future/article/2018 1029-why-the-flu-of-1918-was-so-deadly (accessed December 2021).

4. Lei Zhao, "Rocketship," excerpt used by permission.

5. Ali Watkins et. al., "Top E.R. Doctor Who Treated Virus Patients . . ." *The New York Times*, April 27, 2020. https://www .nytimes.com/2020/04/27/nyregion/new-york-city-doctor -suicide-coronavirus.html (accessed December 2021).

6. Gabrielle Chung, "New York City EMT Dies . . ." People.com, April 27, 2020. https://people.com/human-interest/nyc-emt-dies -apparent-suicide-coronavirus-pandemic/ (accessed December 2021).

7. Gidget Fuentes, "Hospital Ship Comfort Ends NYC COVID-19 Mission After Treating 182 Patients," *USNI News*, April 27, 2020. https://news.usni.org/2020/04/27/hospital-ship-comfort-ends -nyc-covid-19-mission-after-treating-182-patients (accessed December 2021).

Convalescence

1. Stephen Crane, "A Man Said to the Universe," from *War Is Kind &
   Other Lines* (1899).
2. John Bowden, "New York City Sets Record . . ." *The Hill*, May 13,
   2020. https://thehill.com/policy/transportation/497553-new-york
   -city-sets-record-of-58-straight-days-with-no-pedestrian (accessed
   December 2021).

ACKNOWLEDGMENTS

Dad, for my existence, and your penchant for writing diaries that probably passed into my DNA. For taking me to watch all those movies that have become intertwined into a language of how I navigate and write about the world, for telling me you were proud of me right before you would go, for still watching over my shoulder even after you're gone.

Mom, for raising and trying to love me the best way you knew how despite how nearly impossible it was for you at the time, for staying alive and compelling me to witness how life always can find renewed purpose even after tremendous loss and tragedy.

Linus, for already being prepared to be the big brother I always needed fourteen years before I was born, for being the smartest person I know, for teaching me what confidence was in eighth grade after we watched *Pleasantville* together and I asked for help, for letting me list you as my emergency contact when I couldn't trust anyone else, and for not giving up on us after our father died. Thank you for still reminding me to this day he really was proud of me.

Sherry and Karen, for being there at the right time and the right place as I was growing up, ensuring for me that I deserved love before I could know what that was. You righted a ship that didn't even know how to leave the harbor; it would have ultimately sunk without you.

ACKNOWLEDGMENTS

Emily, Edward, Andrew, Gilbert, Auntie Jennifer, Uncle Alfred, Uncle Raymond, and all my extended family, including those no longer with us: As far apart as we are and as little we see one another, you are still and always will be family.

Mel, my rock, my Zen master, my best friend, my lockdown buddy, my partner, my copilot. Thank you for patiently granting me an understanding of what a home and family could be, for loving *all* of me, inspiring me to always *want* to do better simply by being in the presence of your love, let alone being the bedrock for me to comfortably revel in the freedom to dare and to be fully myself, and to explore what and how love is and can become.

Lei, the longest friend I've had, for your genius, for being the better writer I could always look up to, for those long nights staying up and walking city streets while helping me reframe my childhood angst, and for the poem you wrote for me when my father died. For being a best friend.

Mihaela, for being by my side at all the places we've monsooned together, especially after trusting in the machinations of a stranger, and for what turned into an unexpected friendship most people spend entire lives either searching for or never knowing could exist. For your wit that has fed my soul, and for laughing at all of my attempts to match. You exist. We exist. Thank you not only for existing, but for *living.*

Pier, my number one penpal and all our obscure sorrows. You believed in and recognized me as a fellow published author before I did myself. Thank you for sending that email back in 2016 out of the blue to me—then a complete stranger halfway across the world—not knowing where it could lead. Well here it is: This book you hold in your hands is a testament to your faith.

Donna, for being the getaway driver on all the trips you come on, for proofreading beyond even this book, for being more reliable than the little sister from *She's All That.* You are the peaceful warrior I always needed by my side.

Evie Joy, my "beautifully souled former stranger" with that visioneering, wandering heart of wonder and your magical ukulele.

From a random IG Live to redwood forests, railroad stations, campfires, ski slopes, and marinas, thank you for your healing sense of humor and music that found and carried both of us during the pandemic.

Priscilla, for "more than you know," and helping take down the walls of a writer's block like an assassin. For the grace in granting front-row seats to reinvigorated faith and renewed destiny, and the detours toward meaning, whether in rainstorms, round-abouts, or *resfeber*—solve by walking. Trust the process.

Sabrina, for complementing one-armed push-ups side by side and being my burger buddy. For being the first ever to conference-call me hundreds of miles away in the middle of a trip, about a trip. For seeing a twin flame in me.

Kimmy, for that random message out of the blue and letting me play any part in your reawakening for adventure afterward. For the beauty in rupture. For *kintsugi*.

Debashree and the rest of the medical team at Elmhurst Hospital, for taking care of my grandfather since the moment he checked into your ER. I am grateful to have crossed paths and worked with many of you personally during our respective medical careers, and I could not have asked for a better group of people who would be there for him and hold his hand in my stead during his final days.

Diana, my travel ethicist, for checking in on me and taking over my Instagram for a few days during the pandemic just so I could take a break and you could answer countless public health questions from my audience.

Vibhu, from *Faces of the Frontline* to El Camino, for your support to all of us frontline healthcare workers during the pandemic, for your art, your intellect, and the humbling feeling that you would even want me to be part of your journey to make this world a better place.

Christian Franz, for your unprompted genuine enthusiasm in already seeing whatever it is you see in me that I still am struggling to fully see myself.

ACKNOWLEDGMENTS

Valerie, my high school sweetheart, for your summer solstice letter urging me to embrace travel six long years before I finally did. You may not have known it at the time, but you were the first to recognize wanderlust in my potential before anyone else. Thanks for always staying in touch. For never being a stranger.

Cindy, wherever you are, for your leather-bound birthday present of a diary we exchanged back and forth when we were both just thirteen years old. For always writing, let alone teaching me how to write at all.

Amy Sall, for arriving at the right time and place when I needed it, for not only teaching but also *proving* what the bridge of incidents is to me, and helping me confirm something I long had struggled to explain.

Jeffrey, for somehow landing in my life at the right moments to remind me we don't always have to have an answer to the magic out there. Thank you for reminding me to sit back and enjoy the ride.

Shilpa, for checking in once a decade to mark the next big chapters of my life even when for you it's just to "catch up." It's never just a "catch up" on my end. It's you catching me before I fall.

Lisa Ling, for the privilege of trust you've placed in me during the pandemic and graciously accepting to write a foreword that still makes me pinch myself and wonder if it's really about me. For staying in touch since and being there for all of us, especially for all that you have done for us in the Asian American and Pacific Islander community; I can only hope to live up to your legacy.

Justin Lin, for trusting a lanky sixteen-year-old high school kid you never met—who didn't even know what it meant to be Asian American at the time—to co-lead your NYC premiere of *Better Luck Tomorrow* on April 10, 2001 (and for putting up with my angry dad afterward). That day was the beginning of many things for me, not the least of which was recognizing my own potential.

Dr. Stu Weiss, for letting me volunteer for the annual NYC Marathon, my favorite thing to look forward to every year that somehow isn't anything related to travel, for inviting me into your world of event medicine and for seeing potential in what we could do together before I ever could imagine it. When you made sure the races would return, I knew we could still nourish a sense of hope in this pandemic.

Ranya, Christian, and Naina, for bearing witness to my very first monsoon in Egypt before we even called it monsooning.

Avanti, for probably being the first friend to tell me I *should* write a book back in 2006. I know it took sixteen years, but better late than never, no?

Mona, from Machu Picchu to Dubai to Sydney, thank you for being the first to shine a light on the very path that was once too dark for me to see.

Ms. Vento, back at CCB, for teaching me how to write essays when I was ten years old. You gave me a failing score of 4/12 for my first essay, but then you challenged me to never give up. Here's my latest one. I hope it's better than a 4/12.

Trinity, my literary agent, for reaching out of the blue that fresh winter morning and going on a gut feeling, asking to represent me if I was interested in being published. Here we are less than two years later . . . I have yet to meet you in person, but this book you're holding is the hug we're yet to have.

Aly, my writing coach, for taking the time to get to know me and my voice before embracing chaos, and conceiving an order to the narrative that we now hold in our hands.

Andrea, my publisher, for championing my publication and saying all the right things when we first virtually met. Thank you for believing in me and making this process both fun and effortless at the same time.

Mikayla, my copyeditor, for carrying this story into the final stages, and for leaving that little note for me as a way of introducing yourself. Your reassurance and words meant more to me than you know.

MJ Hiblen, for the illustrations that encapsulate all that frustrates us and yet all that gives us hope. For trusting me to write your foreword. If they say a picture is worth a thousand words, yours have been worth countless millions to us. Thank you for ensuring that our efforts, and not the efforts of those who chose to instead stay on the wrong side of history, will be remembered long after we're gone.

Dr. Steve Ko, my buddy from residency, for the handful of well-timed jokes during the pandemic that kept me going.

All my monsooners for believing in me. After my father's death, I yearned for more family. Better late than never.

Sheryl Zhang, Anderson Lee, Donald Lai, Daniel Wong, Alli Zheng, Paul Woo, Kareem Black, Roxanne Menchaca, Katie Li, Chen Yu, Rik Brinks, Paula Cheng, Grace Kelly, Daniela Zarzer, Shenela Lakhani, Norman Chen, Tudor Mustata, Victoria Li, Michael Holder, Chen Yu, Jenny Fu, Claire Webster, Diana Pirrag, Nicolette Columbia, Hanan Abdelrahman, Kateryna Savchenko, Vyjayanthi Vadrevu, Lynn, Michelle, Ana, my remarkable followers on social media, and anyone else I may have forgotten: **my Good Samaritans of the pandemic**. Thank you, thank you, thank you for keeping us alive with all your unsolicited and unexpected efforts of love, guidance, resources, delivery of personal protective equipment, food, cookies, offers of lodging for frontline healthcare workers, admitting my patient transfers, coming into work every day as my rockstar emergency room medical team, making our shifts more bearable, tagging me with well-timed messages of encouragement, and constant reminders of what wonderful things friends can do for one another in times where it can be easy to doubt resolve. This book, my life, wouldn't have made it through the pandemic without you. This book, my life: You're holding it right now in your hands.

ABOUT THE AUTHOR

~~~~~~~~

Dr. Calvin D. Sun is an NYC-based emergency physician. During the COVID-19 pandemic, Dr. Sun worked as an emergency physician and clinical assistant professor in Emergency Medicine in ERs all over New York City and soon gained a substantial online following from sharing his insider experiences and advice. A frequent guest on national and international news programs, he brings medical knowledge and empathy to the story of COVID-19.

Over the past twelve years, Dr. Sun has traveled to more than two hundred countries and territories, while also completing medical school and going through medical residency at the same time. He leads other everyday travelers around the world on memorable adventures with his organization, The Monsoon Diaries (monsoondiaries.com).